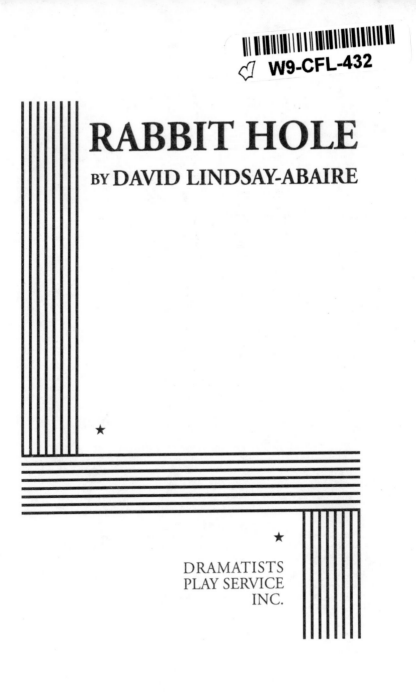

RABBIT HOLE

BY DAVID LINDSAY-ABAIRE

★

★

DRAMATISTS
PLAY SERVICE
INC.

RABBIT HOLE
Copyright © 2006, David Lindsay-Abaire

All Rights Reserved

SPECIAL NOTE

SPECIAL NOTE ON MUSIC

A CD with cue sheet of the sound design and original music by John Gromada is available through the Play Service for $35.00, plus shipping. The nonprofessional fee for the use of this music is $20.00 per performance.

SPECIAL NOTE ON SONGS AND RECORDINGS

For performances of copyrighted songs, arrangements or recordings mentioned in these Plays, the permission of the copyright owner(s) must be obtained. Other songs, arrangements or recordings may be substituted provided permission from the copyright owner(s) of such songs, arrangements or recordings is obtained; or songs, arrangements or recordings in the public domain may be substituted.

RABBIT HOLE was commissioned by South Coast Repertory (Martin Benson, Artistic Director; David Emmes, Producing Artistic Director) in Costa Mesa, CA.

RABBIT HOLE received its world premiere on Broadway at the Biltmore Theatre on January 12, 2006. It was produced by the Manhattan Theatre Club (Lynne Meadow, Artistic Director; Barry Grove, Executive Producer). It was directed by Daniel Sullivan; the set design was by John Lee Beatty; the costume design was by Jennifer Von Mayrhauser; the lighting design was by Christopher Akerlind; the original music and sound design were by John Gromada; and the production stage manager was Roy Harris. The cast was as follows:

BECCA	Cynthia Nixon
IZZY	Mary Catherine Garrison
HOWIE	John Slattery
NAT	Tyne Daly
JASON	John Gallagher, Jr.

CHARACTERS

BECCA — late thirties/early forties
IZZY — early thirties, Becca's sister
HOWIE — late thirties/early forties, Becca's husband
NAT — mid-sixties, Becca and Izzy's mother
JASON — a seventeen-year-old boy

PLACE

Larchmont, New York.

TIME

The present.

RABBIT HOLE

ACT ONE

Scene 1

Late February. A spacious eat-in kitchen. Saturday afternoon. Becca, late thirties, is folding the laundry, kids' clothes, and putting it in neat piles on the table. Her sister, Izzy, early thirties, is in the middle of a story, getting herself a glass of orange juice from the fridge.

IZZY. And then I see her across the bar, coming at me with this *look*, you know. And everybody kinda steps aside for her, like the Red Sea, or whatever — just clears a path for her, and I'm like, "What's with *this* nut job?"

BECCA. But you don't even know this woman.

IZZY. Never seen her before. I was just sitting there with Reema. Do you remember Reema?

BECCA. No.

IZZY. She's a friend of mine. I was sitting there with Reema, and suddenly this lady is in my face. And she's all sweaty and yelling and *really* pissed.

BECCA. Why?

IZZY. I don't even *know* at this point. It has something to do with her boyfriend, who's apparently at the end of the bar.

BECCA. Were you flirting or — ?

IZZY. No, I don't even know who she's *talking* about. So she's all up in my face, and her breath is like —

BECCA. Boozy?

IZZY. Yeah, boozy, but even worse, you know, like there's something rancid stuck to the roof of her mouth.

BECCA. Ew.

[handwritten note: I act upset]

IZZY. Rotting peanut butter or something.

BECCA. Good lord, Izzy.

[handwritten note: great change in action]

IZZY. And she's harassing me, and blowing her stank-breath in my face. And cussing. My God, you wouldn't believe the words that came out of this lady's mouth.

BECCA. And you don't even know who she's talking about.

IZZY. She's talking about her boyfriend.

BECCA. No, I know but —

[handwritten note: Stop]

<u>IZZY. Auggie. *(Beat.)*</u>

BECCA. Oh. I thought you didn't know who she —

IZZY. No, at the *time* I didn't know who she was talking about, because I didn't know he was *there*. But then I figured it out later, "Oh, she must be Auggie's girlfriend."

BECCA. So you know him.

IZZY. Yeah, I know him, but still. Lemme finish.

BECCA. I'm sorry.

IZZY. So she's all, "You bitch, you. Fuck you, you bitch."

BECCA. Izzy —

IZZY. Sorry: "F-u, you b," and all that. Just talking like a maniac.

[handwritten note: say quick]

BECCA. Uh-huh.

IZZY. And people are looking at us, so I'm starting to feel self-conscious.

BECCA. Of course.

IZZY. And she's just going off, and I can't really *do* anything because the place is so crowded, you know? And she's a big lady. Real hefty. More chins than — what does Mom say?

BECCA. More Chins than a Chinese phone book.

IZZY. Exactly. So I can't even get around her to escape or whatever. And I'm starting to feel *violated*, you know?

BECCA. Sure.

IZZY. My personal space, and my dignity, or what have you, so I just made a fist, hauled off, and BOOM! *(Beat.)*

BECCA. What does that mean?

IZZY. It means I hit her.

BECCA. No, you didn't.

IZZY. Crazy, right?

BECCA. You hit her?

IZZY. Yeah. Right in the face. BOOM. She went down.

BECCA. Oh my God, Izzy. You *hit* that woman?

IZZY. I couldn't get around her. And she was screaming like a retard.

6

BECCA. Izzy —

IZZY. What would *you* have done?

BECCA. Well, I certainly wouldn't have hit her. Jesus.

IZZY. And you know what they don't tell ya? It really hurts. To punch someone. It frickin' hurts.

BECCA. Well, yeah.

IZZY. They don't put that on TV. It's all, "Now that oughta show him." But for me it was like, "Mother*fucker,* that *killed!*" Look at my knuckles. *(Shows her; then off Becca's look.)* What?

BECCA. Nothing.

IZZY. You don't approve?

BECCA. I didn't say that.

IZZY. This lady was *at* me.

BECCA. I know. I didn't say anything.

IZZY. But you wanna though. *(Beat.)*

BECCA. I just worry about you.

IZZY. Don't worry about me. *She* was the one on the floor.

BECCA. That's not what I meant. You were in a bar fight.

IZZY. So?

BECCA. A *bar fight,* Izzy.

IZZY. She was up in my face!

BECCA. I know, but it's so …

IZZY. What?

BECCA. *Jerry Springer.*

IZZY. What's that supposed to mean? You think I'm trashy?

BECCA. You punched a woman in the face!

IZZY. She provoked me!

BECCA. Were you drunk?

IZZY. No.

BECCA. I thought you were getting it together.

IZZY. Don't judge me.

BECCA. You said you were gonna take it easy.

IZZY. Man, Becca. Why do you have to — ?

BECCA. You can't be doing this kinda stuff, Izzy. You're not a kid anymore.

IZZY. I didn't realize there was a cut-off date.

BECCA. Well, there should be. For acting like a jackass there *should* be a cut-off date. Were you on anything?

IZZY. Oh my God. Stop

BECCA. Were you?

IZZY. No. Man, why did I say anything to you?

7

BECCA. I don't know. Why *did* you?

IZZY. Look, I went out. I got into a fight. I thought it was a funny story. I thought you'd be amused.

BECCA. I'm not.

IZZY. Clearly.

BECCA. I thought you were gonna go easy, that's all. That you were gonna do less of this.

IZZY. Hey, I'm still coping, too, Becca. I know it's not the same, but it's still hard. Okay? *(Beat.)*

BECCA. Don't do that.

IZZY. Do what?

BECCA. Gimme a break.

IZZY. What? I'm not allowed to be *upset* anymore?

BECCA. No, you're not allowed to *use* him.

IZZY. What are you — ?

BECCA. As an excuse.

IZZY. I'm *not.*

BECCA. You're not allowed to use him to justify your own shit. Just don't do that. Please. *(Silence. Becca folds the clothes.)*

IZZY. That's not what I was doing.

BECCA. Okay.

IZZY. I'm hungry. Mind if I get something?

BECCA. Since when do you ask?

IZZY. You're making me feel sensitive. *(Izzy heads back to the fridge.)* Where's Howie?

BECCA. He's with Rick. They're playing squash.

IZZY. *(Chuckles.)* Squash. *(Regarding something in the fridge.)* What's this? Pudding?

BECCA. It's gonna be crème caramel.

IZZY. Howie's a lucky man. Ya won't see *me* making anyone crème caramel.

BECCA. If you're hungry, Isabel, grab something. Don't stand there with the door open.

IZZY. *(Holds up an individual crème caramel.)* Can I have one of these? There's an extra in here. *(Beat.)*

BECCA. Yeah, okay.

IZZY. Well I won't eat it if you don't want me to.

BECCA. No, go ahead. You're right, there's an extra.

IZZY. You sure?

BECCA. Just let me finish it.

IZZY. I can eat it like this.

BECCA. No. Then it's just custard.

IZZY. I like custard.

BECCA. I didn't make custard, I made crème caramel. *(Becca gets a dessert plate, and over the following she takes the ramekin and runs a knife around the inside edge of it.)* How's work?

IZZY. Don't ask me that, please.

BECCA. Why not? *(Beat.)* You got fired?

IZZY. It never ends with me, does it.

BECCA. Not often, no.

IZZY. Don't tell Mom.

BECCA. How can you get fired from Applebee's?

IZZY. It was all politics. I don't really wanna get into it. *(Becca flips the ramekin over onto the plate, and the crème caramel comes out. She gets a spoon and hands both to Izzy.)* Thank you. *(Becca wipes down the counter, cleans up. Izzy pokes at the caramel with her spoon.)* I like how it oozes.

BECCA. Of course you do.

IZZY. *(Takes a bite.)* Mmmmm.

BECCA. Better than custard, isn't it?

IZZY. Yes, it is. You were right. Again. *(Beat.)* And again and again and again. *(Becca goes back to folding clothes.)* I wasn't using him as an excuse. I was just saying that it's been hard to pull it together, that's all. For all of us.

BECCA. Izzy, please.

IZZY. And I *wasn't* drinking when I hit that lady. Stone sober.

BECCA. Yeah *right*.

IZZY. I *was*. I just had soda that night. *(We hear the dryer buzz.)*

BECCA. She gonna press charges, ya think?

IZZY. No, Auggie would kill her. She's over it anyway. She moved out. Went to her cousin's or something. *(Becca, on her way to the laundry room, stops.)*

BECCA. What are you talking about?

IZZY. She moved. Out of Auggie's place. They're not together anymore.

BECCA. *(Confused; comes back.)* I'm sorry … Do you *know* these people?

IZZY. Auggie I do. The girlfriend I only *heard* about. *(Beat.)*

BECCA. What'd you do, Izzy?

IZZY. Whadaya mean?

BECCA. To that woman. What'd you *do* to her?

IZZY. I told you, I hit her.

9

BECCA. *Before* that.

IZZY. Nothing. That was the first time I met her.

BECCA. People don't scream in your face for no reason.

IZZY. Sure they do. You should get out more.

BECCA. Were you sleeping with him? This Auggie guy, whatever his name is? You were sleeping with him, right? *(Beat.)*

IZZY. Where ya goin' with this?

BECCA. Well Jesus, Iz, you tell this story like you're an innocent bystander. You say you don't know *who* this woman was —

IZZY. I didn't!

BECCA. You were having sex with her boyfriend!

IZZY. That is so beside the point!

BECCA. It *is?!*

IZZY. It was over between them for a long time. They were just living together because of the rent situation. She didn't care what he did.

BECCA. Then why did she accost you in a crowded bar?

IZZY. Because she's a lunatic! *(Beat.)* And Auggie told her I was pregnant.

BECCA. Why would he — ? *(Stops mid-sentence, then realizes ...)* Oh my God, Izzy.

IZZY. I know, right?

BECCA. You are *not*. *(Izzy just shrugs, "Whadaya gonna do?" Becca is not pleased.)* Oh my God.

IZZY. He's a really good guy, Bec. You're gonna like him. He's a musician.

BECCA. *(Oozing irony.)* That's terrific.

IZZY. No, not like you think. He gets work. He's a *working* musician.

BECCA. Is that why you're here? To tell me you're pregnant?

IZZY. Pretty much.

BECCA. I knew something was up. You're not one to pop by on a Saturday afternoon.

IZZY. I pop by.

BECCA. How long have you known?

IZZY. A few weeks.

BECCA. And you're just telling me now?

IZZY. Well, Jesus, Bec ...

BECCA. What? You didn't wanna tell me?

IZZY. No.

BECCA. Why not?

10

IZZY. Why do you *think? (Beat.)* God, everything's so fucked up.

BECCA. Does Mom know?

IZZY. Yeah.

BECCA. You told Mom before me?

IZZY. I *had* to.

BECCA. Oh my God, Izzy.

IZZY. Stop saying that.

BECCA. What are you gonna do?

IZZY. Well, I'm gonna keep it, if that's what you're asking. *(Beat.)* Auggie wants to, too. We're excited about it. This is exactly the kind of thing that gives a person clarity. *(Beat.)*

BECCA. Izzy ...

IZZY. Look, I'm sure this is really hard for you, for a bunch of reasons, but can I just say...? I don't need any advice right now. Or any lectures or whatever it is you're composing inside your head at the moment. I just need you to pretend to be happy for me. Okay? Even if you don't feel that right now. I'd like you to pretend that you do. All right? *(Pause.)*

BECCA. Well ... of *course* I'm happy for you. I was just taken aback. If you think a baby is gonna ... fulfill you, or give you clarity or whatever, then, obviously it's a wonderful thing. I *am* happy for you. I don't need to *pretend.* Jesus, Izzy, gimme some credit. *(Izzy hugs her sister.)*

IZZY. Thank you. *(Silence. Becca looks at the stacks of folded kids' clothes.)*

BECCA. Well I should probably hold off on this then.

IZZY. What do you mean?

BECCA. I'm washing all these clothes to give to Goodwill. I might as well save them for you. In case you have a boy. No sense in my giving these away. *(Izzy looks from Becca to the clothes. Piles of little pants and shirts and balled-up socks. They're all clothes a four-year-old might wear. Izzy looks uneasy.)*

IZZY. I don't know, Bec. They're in baby clothes for so long, it'd be a few years before he could even fit into this stuff.

BECCA. It comes up very quickly. You wouldn't even believe it.

IZZY. Plus we don't have a lot of room to ...

BECCA. That's okay. I'll keep them here. In the basement. You'll be happy I saved them.

IZZY. But what if it's a girl?

BECCA. Then I'll bring them down to Goodwill. What's the big deal? You're gonna thank me. A couple years' worth of free clothes here. Think of the money you're gonna save.

IZZY. It's not about the money.

BECCA. Well it *should* be. You need to start thinking about stuff like that, Iz. Especially if the dad's a musician. It costs a lot to raise a child.

IZZY. It'd be weird, that's all. If it's a boy. To see him running around in Danny's clothes. *(Beat.)* I would feel weird. You would, too, I think. *(Beat.)* I'm sorry.

BECCA. No, *I'm* sorry. Of course it'd be weird. I don't know what I was —

IZZY. It was a nice offer. I just —

BECCA. You'll get a lot of clothes anyway. Christmas and birthdays. You won't have to worry about that.

IZZY. No, I know, but —

BECCA. It would be one thing if they were hand-me-downs but —

IZZY. Exactly. *(Pause. Becca goes back to folding.)*

BECCA. It's probably a girl anyway.

IZZY. You think?

BECCA. I'm definitely getting a girl vibe. I'm a little psychic about this stuff.

IZZY. Oh yeah?

BECCA. Remember I said Debbie was having a girl.

IZZY. You did.

BECCA. And Karen?

IZZY. Karen too, I remember.

BECCA. I think there's a girl in there.

IZZY. I hope there is. That's what I want. I mean, either way, so long as it's healthy obviously, but if I had to pick, I hope it's a girl.

BECCA. Me, too. *(Beat.)* What'd Mom say?

IZZY. She was happy. *(Beat.)*

BECCA. Really?

IZZY. I know. I thought she'd lay into me but …

BECCA. Huh. *(Becca clears Izzy's crème caramel plate, and brings it to the sink.)*

IZZY. Thanks for the crème caramel.

BECCA. Sure. *(Beat.)*

IZZY. I'm sorry, Bec. If this is hard. I know the timing really sucks.

BECCA. Hey. What can ya do? *(Beat.)* I'm glad you told me. *(Beat.)* And I'm really happy for you. *(The lights fade.)*

Scene 2

Becca and Howie's living room, later that night. Dessert has moved in here. They're finishing up their crème caramels, chatting.

BECCA. Ridiculous, right? Nine weeks pregnant. In a bar. Drinking.

HOWIE. You said she *wasn't* drinking.

BECCA. No, *she* said. But you know Izzy. Plus the place was probably *clogged* with cigarette smoke.

HOWIE. Not anymore. Clean Indoor Air Act.

BECCA. She was in *Yonkers.* You think they enforce that in Yonkers?

HOWIE. I wouldn't worry about it. If the babies in France turn out okay, I'm sure this one'll be fine, too.

BECCA. You think this is funny, Howie?

HOWIE. Of course not. But you need to relax about it. Izzy could be right.

BECCA. About what?

HOWIE. The baby getting her on track. It can wake a person up. It did us.

BECCA. She was bragging about a *bar* fight.

HOWIE. It wasn't a bar fight.

BECCA. They were in a *bar. Fighting.*

HOWIE. Izzy hit someone, she didn't get into a fight. Blows were never exchanged.

BECCA. What is your point? It's okay for a pregnant woman to be punching people?

HOWIE. Well, so long as they don't punch her back, it's probably all right.

BECCA. What are you — ? Why are you defending her?

HOWIE. I'm not. I just think it's silly to get worked up about it.

BECCA. I'm not worked up. I'm just saying.

HOWIE. You're right, it's a mess, but what can we do? Maybe it'll be fine. Izzy's not a moron. *(Off her look.)* Okay, she *acts* like one sometimes but … A baby can be good for a person.

BECCA. I know that, Howie.

HOWIE. All right then. *(Beat.)* This was good. The crème caramel.

13

BECCA. Thank you. Izzy tried to eat one upside down. *(Becca clears the crème caramel dishes. She brings them into the kitchen.)*

HOWIE. You want more wine?

BECCA. *(From the kitchen.)* No, I've had two already.

HOWIE. Half a glass, I wanna empty this bottle. *(He empties the rest into her glass.)*

BECCA. Mom's thrilled, by the way.

HOWIE. She called?

BECCA. Izzy must've told her I knew.

HOWIE. And how was that?

BECCA. What, two hours on the phone with *Mom?* *(Howie lowers the lights in the room as Becca reenters.)* What are you doing?

HOWIE. My eyes are sore, staring at that computer all day. *(Becca settles onto the couch with her wine.)*

BECCA. You think this means she wants baby stuff? For her birthday? Maternity clothes or something?

HOWIE. *(Joins her on the couch.)* No, wait for the baby shower. Just get whatever you were gonna get her.

BECCA. Good, because I was gonna buy her a bathroom set.

HOWIE. A what?

BECCA. A bathroom set. Shower curtain, bath mat … a little skirt for the sink. They sell them as sets.

HOWIE. This is for Izzy's birthday?

BECCA. The last time I was there, you should've seen her bathroom. It looked like a frat boy decorated.

HOWIE. Huh.

BECCA. What?

HOWIE. It just seems like a funny gift. A bath mat.

BECCA. It's the whole set, Howie.

HOWIE. No, I know. Still.

BECCA. I thought it'd be nice.

HOWIE. It *is* nice. But maybe she'd rather have perfume or something.

BECCA. Izzy doesn't wear perfume.

HOWIE. No, I know, but —

BECCA. I was trying to be practical.

HOWIE. Okay.

BECCA. It's a good gift. I'd like it if someone gave it to me.

HOWIE. I'll make note of that for Christmas.

BECCA. You think it's dumb.

HOWIE. No, get her the sink skirt, the set-thingy whatever.

14

BECCA. Bathroom set.

HOWIE. Get her that if you think she'll like it.

BECCA. I'm gonna.

HOWIE. Great. She'll love it.

BECCA. You should've just said that to begin with.

HOWIE. Yeah, I know. Now. *(Howie looks at her and smiles. She smiles back. A moment passes between them.)*

BECCA. How was squash?

HOWIE. Good. I lost but it was good.

BECCA. How's Rick?

HOWIE. Rick's fine.

BECCA. And Debbie?

HOWIE. Debbie wasn't there.

BECCA. I know, but did Rick mention her?

HOWIE. Not really. I guess she took the kids to her mother's this weekend.

BECCA. Rick didn't wanna go?

HOWIE. He has work.

BECCA. How *are* the kids?

HOWIE. Fine, I guess. He said that Robbie's doing T-ball now, and Emily has mastered the plié. *(Beat.)* Anything else?

BECCA. No, that's it.

HOWIE. You can call her, you know. You can call Debbie and ask her these questions yourself.

BECCA. I don't wanna call her. She should call me.

HOWIE. Okay.

BECCA. Why can't *she* call *me?*

HOWIE. I don't know.

BECCA. No?

HOWIE. She's uncomfortable, Bec.

BECCA. Is that what Rick said?

HOWIE. Rick didn't say anything. But obviously if she hasn't called you, it's because she doesn't know what to say.

BECCA. How about, "Hey, Becca, how you doing? Haven't seen you in a while."

HOWIE. If you're pissed, you should call her and tell her.

BECCA. No, Howie, it's her job to call me.

HOWIE. Okay.

BECCA. I would've been there for her if God forbid something had ever happened to Robbie or Em. I wouldn't have vanished the way she did.

HOWIE. People get weird, you know that. It's probably hard for her.

BECCA. Hard for *her?*

HOWIE. I'm just saying. Look at my brother. Spent the whole funeral talking about the Mets. Obviously he couldn't deal. He'd talk about anything *but* Danny. And that's my brother.

BECCA. Yeah, well, your brother's an asshole. *(Beat.)* I should drop her a note.

HOWIE. Maybe you should.

BECCA. "Dear Debbie — just so's ya know, accidents aren't contagious."

HOWIE. Okay, let it go.

BECCA. Let what go?

HOWIE. Whatever's making you tense. You should try to relax a little.

BECCA. I *am* relaxed.

HOWIE. We'll see. *(Howie grabs a remote and clicks on the stereo. A song like Al Green's "Livin' for You" plays quietly.*)*

BECCA. Oh jeez, Howie.

HOWIE. What? It's chill music. You need it. Now turn around.

BECCA. For what?

HOWIE. Just face that way. *(She does. He moves in to massage her shoulders.)* Thank you. *(Massages her.)* See? Your shoulders are all knotted up.

BECCA. Yeah, well ...

HOWIE. Forget about Debbie and Izzy and whoever else is bugging you.

BECCA. *She* has no idea, by the way. Izzy. *No* idea what she's getting into.

HOWIE. *(Massaging her.)* I know.

BECCA. Do you remember how exhausted we were? The feedings at all hours. The sleep deprivation. Do you think Izzy's ready for that? The utter torture of it all?

HOWIE. Enough about Izzy.

BECCA. I'm sorry. But she's a sleeper. Izzy *needs* sleep more than other people. You talk about wake-up call or whatever you were saying, well, she's gonna *get* one, big time. *(Howie continues to massage her. Becca seems to warm up to it.)*

HOWIE. Maybe we should go somewhere. A cruise or something. You need to be pampered.

---

* See Special Note on Songs and Recordings on copyright page.

BECCA. You've taken off enough time as it is.

HOWIE. I'll talk to Alan. What's another week? I can handle most of my accounts from out of town anyway. *(He kisses her neck.)*

BECCA. What are you doing?

HOWIE. I'm kissing your neck.

BECCA. Why?

HOWIE. I'm trying to relax you.

BECCA. Uh-huh.

HOWIE. Something wrong with that?

BECCA. I see what this is. Dimming the lights.

HOWIE. What? I can't massage my wife?

BECCA. *(Giggles a little.)* You don't have eye strain.

HOWIE. So?

BECCA. "Oh, I've been staring at that computer all day."

HOWIE. Well I *do* stare at that computer all day.

BECCA. You're trying to seduce me.

HOWIE. Am I?

BECCA. Plying me with liquor.

HOWIE. It worked in college.

BECCA. All right, Romeo.

HOWIE. What?

BECCA. *(Pushing him away playfully.)* That's enough.

HOWIE. Why?

BECCA. You're being very naughty.

HOWIE. Naughty's good. You used to like naughty. *(She gets up from the couch.)* Where are you going?

BECCA. I still have stuff to bag up.

HOWIE. Are you kidding?

BECCA. No, there are piles of clothes up there, Howie.

HOWIE. Well, if they've waited *this* long.

BECCA. I wanted to get it done.

HOWIE. We'll get it done tomorrow. I'll pitch in.

BECCA. Yeah, right.

HOWIE. I will.

BECCA. Uh-huh.

HOWIE. Becca …

BECCA. I'm sorry. I'm feeling kinda antsy tonight. You're right, the Izzy stuff got under my skin.

HOWIE. Right. *(He clicks the music off. Pause.)*

BECCA. So, what, you're gonna pout now?

HOWIE. Well Jesus, Bec …

BECCA. Jesus, *what?*

HOWIE. It's been almost eight months. *(Beat.)*

BECCA. But who's keeping track?

HOWIE. I am. I'm keeping track. *(Beat.)* I'm sorry. *(Off her look.)* What? That makes me perverted? Wanting to have sex with my wife?

BECCA. I didn't say that.

HOWIE. Well, you give me these looks like I should feel guilty.

BECCA. Funny, I've been getting the same looks from you.

HOWIE. When have I ever made you feel guilty?

BECCA. I'm just not ready yet, Howie. I'm sorry if you think that's abnormal.

HOWIE. I don't.

BECCA. Then what's the problem here?

HOWIE. We're *never* gonna be ready.

BECCA. If this is just about the sex, Howie —

HOWIE. It's not *just* about the sex.

BECCA. No, then what else is this?

HOWIE. It's also … about … I don't know. Maybe it *is* just the sex. I don't even know honestly. But we're not gonna suddenly wake up one day and be back where we were.

BECCA. I know that.

HOWIE. So we need to … head in that direction at least. Which will feel strange for a while, but …

BECCA. But you wanna have sex.

HOWIE. Don't say it like that.

BECCA. Why not?

HOWIE. Because it sounds crass and selfish.

BECCA. Well, considering everything else — the fact that Danny died, for example — don't you think maybe it *is* a little crass and selfish? For you to be roping me into sex when I don't wanna have it?

HOWIE. I wasn't *roping* you into anything. *Jesus.*

BECCA. No? Al Green isn't roping?

HOWIE. No.

BECCA. *Al Green.*

HOWIE. I thought it was nice. That's all. I was trying to make things nice.

BECCA. Well … you can't. I'm sorry. But things aren't "nice" anymore. *(Pause.)*

HOWIE. I think you should see someone. I know you're not one for therapists, but I think you should. We could go together if

18

that'd help. Or maybe you could try the group again.

BECCA. No.

HOWIE. There are a couple new parents now. It's changed the dynamic a little.

BECCA. We've had this discussion, Howie.

HOWIE. Fine, a psychiatrist then. Someone to talk to. *(Pause.)* No? Yes? Do you have an opinion?

BECCA. I think we should sell the house. *(Beat.)*

HOWIE. Come on, Becca, what?

BECCA. I've been thinking about it for a while, and since we're on the topic —

HOWIE. How were we on the topic?

BECCA. I think it'd help if we moved.

HOWIE. I don't wanna move.

BECCA. He's everywhere, Howie. Everywhere I look, I still see Danny.

HOWIE. We love this house.

BECCA. I can't move without — I mean, Jesus, look at this. *(Grabs a spiky toy dinosaur from nearby.)* Everywhere. Do you even know? *(Grabs a kids' book from a stack of magazines.)* Here: *Runaway Bunny* for godsake. The puzzles. The smudgy fingerprints on the doorjambs.

HOWIE. I like seeing his fingerprints.

BECCA. Because you don't have to sit and stare at them day in and day out. You get to escape. You get to go to work.

HOWIE. Well, if you want to go back to work, Becca —

BECCA. I don't.

HOWIE. — you can call up Sotheby's.

BECCA. No, I can't. That's not who I am anymore. I left all that to be a mom.

HOWIE. Well …

BECCA. Well what? Well, that didn't work out?

HOWIE. I didn't say that.

BECCA. Then what?

HOWIE. If that's the issue —

BECCA. If *what's* the issue?

HOWIE. — then … maybe we should try again. *(Beat.)*

BECCA. Oh for godsakes, Howie …

HOWIE. What? I'm only saying.

BECCA. Is that … Is *that* what this was?

HOWIE. No. No, of course not. It just … it might be something to talk about at some point.

BECCA. I ... I can't. I'm sorry. I can't have that talk.

HOWIE. Okay. (*They are silent, then Becca heads for the stairs. She stops and turns back.*)

BECCA. Look, maybe ... maybe we can consider it at least. The house? (*Beat.*)

HOWIE. Yeah. we'll consider it.

BECCA. Thank you. (*Becca heads upstairs with the dinosaur and the book. Howie watches her go. He sits alone for a couple beats. Then he gets up and goes to the TV cabinet. He rummages around quietly, looking through videotapes. He finally finds what he's looking for. He glances up the stairs, then pops the video in. He shuts off the lights, then sits and watches, the light from the TV flickering on his face. He's watched this tape dozens of times. He doesn't tear up. He just watches it, occasionally smiling at something he hears. The volume is low, but we can hear some of it.*)

VOICE OF DANNY. Now can I?

VOICE OF HOWIE. Let me just get the dog. Taz, lay down. (*On the video, we hear a dog barking and whining a little over this.*)

VOICE OF DANNY. Ready?

VOICE OF HOWIE. Hold on. Taz, down!

VOICE OF DANNY. Lay down, Taz!

VOICE OF HOWIE. I got him. Quick now, before he gets up. Come on, come on ... (*Danny comes running.*) Aaaaand ...

VOICE OF DANNY. Geronimo!

VOICE OF HOWIE. Good job!

VOICE OF DANNY. Did you see me, Daddy?

VOICE OF HOWIE. I did.

VOICE OF DANNY. No, you didn't. I'm invisible.

VOICE OF HOWIE. Ohhh. (*Becca's shadow appears at the top of the stairs, unseen by Howie. She listens for a couple beats.*)

VOICE OF DANNY. I have magic.

VOICE OF HOWIE. Oh, I didn't realize.

VOICE OF DANNY. Do you wanna be invisible?

VOICE OF HOWIE. Okay.

VOICE OF DANNY. Pfffffhhh.

VOICE OF HOWIE. Is that it? Am I invisible?

VOICE OF DANNY. Yeah. I made you invisible. (*Becca's shadow slips away from the stairs.*)

VOICE OF HOWIE. Do you see me?

VOICE OF DANNY. Yeah.

VOICE OF HOWIE. No, you don't. I'm invisible.
VOICE OF DANNY. But I can still see you because I have magic.
VOICE OF HOWIE. Ohhh.
VOICE OF DANNY. Did you forget that part?
VOICE OF HOWIE. Yeah, I forgot that part. *(The lights fade on Howie, watching the video.)*

Scene 3

The eat-in kitchen. A week later. Evening. Becca, Izzy and Nat, their mom, are gathered around a birthday cake, singing. Nat has a glass of wine.

NAT and BECCA. *(End of the song.)* "Happy birthday, dear Isabel … Happy birthday to you … "
NAT. Blow 'em out. *(Izzy blows out the candles. Ad-lib yays and clapping. Becca goes to get a knife.)*
BECCA. What'd you wish for?
IZZY. I can't *say. (Regarding the cake.)* It looks good, Becca.
NAT. Where'd you buy it?
BECCA. I didn't. I made it.
NAT. Of course you did. What a stupid question. Of course you made it.
BECCA. *(Catches Izzy scooping off the frosting.)* Izzy —
IZZY. It's *my* cake.
BECCA. Well, let me cut it first. Watch your fingers. *(Becca cuts slices of cake and puts them on plates over the following. Howie enters with a couple papers.)*
HOWIE. You didn't wait for me?
BECCA. You said not to.
HOWIE. I didn't *mean* it though.
NAT. I tried to stop them, Howie.
IZZY. I wanted cake.
HOWIE. Rude.
BECCA. I didn't know how long you were gonna be up there. Once you get on that computer …
NAT. Did you get it?

21

HOWIE. Yeah, right here. *(Hands her papers.)*

NAT. Let me get my glasses. *(Gets her glasses from her purse.)*

BECCA. *(To Howie.)* Did you have to?

HOWIE. She wanted me to look it up.

BECCA. Any excuse to escape for ten minutes.

IZZY. *(Regarding Nat.)* Well, do you blame him?

NAT. *(Regarding printout.)* What *is* this?

IZZY. Mom, cake.

HOWIE. It's a timeline, starting with the lobotomy. The plane crashes. It's the whole list. It's long.

NAT. Well, still, that doesn't make it a curse.

BECCA. Nobody said it was a curse, Mother.

NAT. Everybody says. That was my point. *Everybody* says it's a curse.

BECCA. Well, nobody in this room.

NAT. You know what it is, really? Hype. Perpetuating the myth. That whole American royalty crap.

IZZY. It's good cake.

NAT. But the Kennedys aren't cursed. They're just really unlucky. And kinda stupid, a lot of them.

HOWIE. Cut me a piece, wouldja, Bec?

NAT. Too much money, that's their curse. And too much time on their hands. If they had to go to work, like normal people, then most of those Kennedys would still be alive.

IZZY. Thanks, Howie. I'm so glad you went and got that timeline.

NAT. Maybe if they had stayed home and watched television once in a while, instead of zipping off to Vail, then none of that stuff would've happened.

BECCA. You have the most interesting theories.

NAT. Don't patronize me.

BECCA. I'm not. I was being serious.

IZZY. *(Regarding cake.)* This is so good.

NAT. Normal people don't fly around in their own planes, for example. I don't know anyone with his own plane, do you? Do you, Howie?

HOWIE. Well, yeah, I know *one* guy but —

NAT. Well, *you* know someone, but that's not the norm. An average person doesn't own an airplane.

HOWIE. No, you're right, he's not average.

BECCA. He's a member of the jet set.

NAT. Exactly! That's what that word means! The jet set. Jet setters! Buzzing around in little Pipers or whatever, crashing off the coast of Massachusetts. Regular people don't have ten relatives die in separate plane wrecks.

HOWIE. It's not ten.

NAT. Just about, if you count Teddy who survived his.

IZZY. Well, I think it's sad.

BECCA. Teddy surviving?

NAT. Well of course it's *sad*. All those good-looking people falling out of the sky like that. It's a frickin' waste. But it isn't a curse. It's just rich people acting stupid.

BECCA. I thought you liked JFK?

NAT. I'm not talking about JFK. I'm not talking about the ones who were *assassinated*. Although getting shot by a crazed gunman is kinda a rich-guy problem too, isn't it?

HOWIE. Well, not *necessarily*.

NAT. It doesn't matter, that's not who I'm talking about. I'm talking about the unqualified *pilots*. I'm talking about playing football. And skiing. At the *same* time!

IZZY. That *was* stupid.

NAT. "Hey, look at me! I'm a Kennedy! I can catch a ball while flying down a mountain on sticks!" Of *course* he died. Idiot. And I know that's a terrible thing to say, but this was a grown man acting like a moron. The arrogance of these people.

HOWIE. The Greeks would call that hubris. "Arrogance in the face of ... " It might not technically be hubris actually.

NAT. If hubris means reckless, then that's right.

HOWIE. No, it doesn't mean reckless. It's more about the gods.

NAT. That's probably the right word then. They're *very* Catholic, those Kennedys.

HOWIE. Now I'm curious, I'm gonna look it up. *(Goes to find dictionary.)*

NAT. *(Regarding wine bottle.)* Fill me up, wouldja Becca? *(Becca reluctantly refills her glass.)* Isn't this nice? Sitting around talking politics? I never do this. It's a nice change. *(Becca turns to pour Izzy some wine. Izzy puts her hand over the glass.)*

IZZY. It's juice. I'm drinking juice.

BECCA. Right, sorry.

IZZY. That's the third time you've done that.

BECCA. I know, I'm sorry.

IZZY. Are you testing me, Becca?

BECCA. No, I'm not testing you. It's just habit. I'm sorry.

HOWIE. *(With dictionary.)* Here it is: "Hubris, an insolent pride or presumption."

NAT. That's them all right. Insolent pride.

HOWIE. And number two is: "In Greek tragedy, arrogance toward the gods leading to nemesis."

IZZY. It's like coming to school when we visit you two.

HOWIE. Is that right?

BECCA. Izzy hated school.

IZZY. No, I didn't. Don't listen to her, Howie. I liked school. Just because I was lousy at it didn't mean I hated it.

BECCA. Sounds like you and squash, Howie.

HOWIE. *(To Izzy.)* She means the game, not the vegetable.

IZZY. I knew what she meant.

NAT. You know who *was* cursed? *Rose* Kennedy. A hundred and four years old. Living through all that death, one after another. *She's* the one I feel sorry for. *(Beat.)*

BECCA. Anyone want more cake?

HOWIE. None for me.

BECCA. We should do gifts then.

IZZY. Yay! Gifts!

NAT. I don't know how I got on all that Kennedy stuff. What was I talking about before?

HOWIE. Aristotle Onassis.

NAT. Oh right, that makes sense. What was I saying about him?

IZZY. You were saying how he'd get really tipsy and never stop talking.

NAT. *(Laughs.)* You bitch. I'm not tipsy. I'm sure I had a very interesting point to make. *(Becca hands a big present to Izzy.)*

BECCA. This is from us.

IZZY. Wow. Thank you.

HOWIE. Happy birthday.

IZZY. It's wrapped so nice. It's a shame to rip it open.

NAT. Becca always makes such nice bows. I don't have the patience. My fingers are too fat. *(Izzy unwraps a very tasteful bathroom set.)* Ohh, look at that.

BECCA. It's more of a practical gift, but I thought you could use it.

HOWIE. It's a bathroom set.

IZZY. I see. It's nice.

NAT. Look at the colors. So pretty.

BECCA. The gift receipt's inside if you want a different style.

NAT. Why would she want a different style? It's beautiful. Isn't it beautiful?

IZZY. Is this your way of telling me you don't like my Three Stooges shower curtain?

BECCA. Of course not.

IZZY. Okay.

BECCA. This is for when you want a change, you'll have it.

NAT. That Three Stooges thing *is* kinda goofy, honey.

IZZY. The word is kitschy, Mother.

NAT. Look up kitschy, wouldja Howie? See if it says crap?

BECCA. I didn't know what to get you.

IZZY. This is great. Seriously, thank you.

BECCA. I *like* your shower curtain.

IZZY. I know, I was kidding.

NAT. And since you're moving in with Auggie —

IZZY. That's right. His bathroom needs a little froofing up. Thank you.

BECCA. You're welcome.

IZZY. Thanks, Howie.

HOWIE. *(Chuckles a little.)* Don't thank me. Becca picked it out. *(Off Becca's look.)* What?

NAT. Okay, now me. *(Hands Izzy an envelope.)*

IZZY. Oooh, an envelope. Smells like cash.

NAT. You *wish*. You think I'm gonna trust you with cash? It's a gift certificate.

IZZY. *(Opens it.)* To A Pea in the Pod!

NAT. They have very nice maternity clothes. Nothing schlubby.

IZZY. Thank you, Mommy. *(Hugs her. Beat.)*

BECCA. I thought we weren't doing baby stuff.

NAT. Who said that?

BECCA. For the birthday. I thought we'd wait until the shower.

NAT. I'll get her something else for the shower. What's the difference?

BECCA. Nothing, I just would've gotten her something different had I known we were doing baby stuff.

HOWIE. That's my fault. I told her to —

NAT. It's *not* baby stuff, it's mommy stuff. She's gonna need clothes.

BECCA. I know, that's why —

IZZY. This is perfect, Bec. I needed a bathroom set.

BECCA. I know you did, but you need baby stuff more.

HOWIE. So take it back. We can take it back.

IZZY. Don't tell her that.

BECCA. No, he's right. I should.

IZZY. Becca, please.

BECCA. I'll get you a basket of Mustela lotions instead. They prevent stretch marks. *(Becca tries to take the bathroom set back. She and Izzy struggle over it for a beat.)*

IZZY. Becca, *let go.* I *like* the bathroom set. You can get the lotions another time. *(Becca lets go, a little embarrassed.)*

BECCA. Okay.

IZZY. Thank you.

NAT. It's a nice set. I like the colors.

HOWIE. More juice, Izzy?

IZZY. No, I'm good. *(They sit in silence for a couple beats.)*

NAT. So can anyone use those stretch-mark lotions, or just pregnant ladies?

HOWIE. Hey, how's Taz?

NAT. He's good. The vet says he needs to lose some weight though.

HOWIE. Really?

NAT. Yeah, he eats like a trouper.

HOWIE. What are you feeding him?

NAT. Just regular dog food. Whatever's on sale.

HOWIE. Oh. Because I wrote down the name of what he usually eats on that printout I gave you. Do you still have that printout?

NAT. Yeah.

HOWIE. We were feeding him Science Diet. They have this special low-fat mix.

NAT. Oh, that stuff's so expensive though. He likes what I've been giving him.

HOWIE. Except it makes him fat.

BECCA. Howie —

NAT. He's not fat. He's just a little chubbier.

IZZY. I think the weight suits him.

NAT. Maybe he eats too much because he feels punished. That's what *I* do. *(Beat.)* I think he misses you.

IZZY. Remember Pickles? Now *she* was fat. *(To Howie.)* That was our dog growing up. She was this enormous … I don't even *know* what. *(To Becca.)* What breed was Pickles?

BECCA. She was a mutt.

IZZY. No, I know, but she was mostly collie I think, with some German shepherd mixed in. Remember how fat she was?

HOWIE. Probably because of what you fed her.

IZZY. Well, yeah, probably.

NAT. Now I remember what it was. What I was gonna say about Aristotle Onassis.

IZZY. Mom, do you have to — ?

NAT. It was about his son, the one who died in the plane crash.

BECCA. I'm gonna wrap up the cake for you. *(She does.)*

NAT. I know — another rich kid in a plane crash — but this was my whole point. You should've stopped me from going off on that Kennedy tangent, because my point was about Onassis, and how when his son died, he was so distraught by the senselessness of it all, that he put up this big reward to anyone who could prove that someone had sabotaged the plane. Have you read this, Howie?

HOWIE. I'm not sure.

NAT. He just couldn't accept that what had happened was an accident, so he offered all this money to anyone who could give him a reasonable explanation. He needed someone to blame.

BECCA. *(To herself, while wrapping the cake.)* Aw, Jesus. Here we go.

NAT. He needed a *reason* for losing his son. But it didn't come of course. And it killed him. The grief did. He only lasted a couple years after that. Because he never came to terms with it. There was nothing to give him comfort, and so he died. You see? *(Becca turns to face her.)* He would rather his son have been killed by some kind of secret assassination than by bad luck. It's like the Kennedy curse, isn't it? People want things to make sense.

BECCA. We don't think Danny died because of a curse, Mom.

NAT. Of course not.

BECCA. Or because someone sabotaged us, or was out to get us. We know there's no sensible explanation.

NAT. I know you do.

BECCA. Then why are you telling this story?

NAT. I'm just talking. I can't talk?

BECCA. You never *just talk*. It *sounds* like you're just talking but it's always so much more, isn't it.

NAT. I don't even know what that means.

IZZY. Hey, here's an idea, let's change the subject.

BECCA. *(To Howie.)* Didn't I say no wine?

HOWIE. She brought it herself, what was I supposed to do?

NAT. What'd I say?

IZZY. Mom, you promised.

NAT. Promised what? It's not my fault she missed my point.

BECCA. What point? That Aristotle Onassis died of grief because he couldn't find someone to *blame?*

NAT. I'm not talking about blame, I'm talking about comfort.

BECCA. Ohhh, comfort. Well then.

27

IZZY. You guys, this is supposed to be my party.

NAT. Where are you getting it?

BECCA. Comfort?

NAT. Yes, if I may ask.

BECCA. I'm not.

NAT. Well.

BECCA. Well what?

NAT. Well, I think you should.

BECCA. Okay. I'll get right on that then. See what I can dig up on eBay.

NAT. Don't get flip, Becca. I'm just trying to talk to you.

IZZY. I'm gonna clean up, because I think we're just about done here.

NAT. Howie says you won't go to the support group. *(Beat.)*

BECCA. Oh. Howie said.

HOWIE. She was asking how you were doing.

BECCA. Why didn't you just say fine? You know she's gonna run with whatever you give her.

NAT. I always thought talk was healthy. Isn't that what all the books say, Howie?

BECCA. So this is what exactly, an intervention?

IZZY. If it is, then I'm really pissed.

HOWIE. It's not an intervention.

NAT. We're just having a discussion.

IZZY. You couldn't wait until tomorrow? It had to happen on my birthday?

HOWIE. Izzy, please.

NAT. I remember when Arthur died, I found the support group very helpful.

BECCA. Well, that's you. It isn't me. And Arthur isn't Danny.

NAT. I'm not saying he is. I'm just saying it was helpful.

HOWIE. She doesn't like the people.

BECCA. Howie —

HOWIE. What? You *don't*. I was just explaining.

NAT. What's wrong with the people? They've lost children, too. They understand what you're going through.

BECCA. No, they don't. They understand what *they're* going through.

NAT. Still, you must have things in common.

BECCA. You would think so, Mother, but actually we don't. Other than that dead kid thing, of course.

28

NAT. It can't hurt to give it another try, Becca.

BECCA. Actually, it *can*. You haven't met that room full of God freaks.

HOWIE. They're not God freaks.

BECCA. Most of them *are*, Howie. That's all they talk about. God's plan. "At least he's in a better place."

HOWIE. They're not all like that.

BECCA. My favorite is: "God needed another angel." What is *that?* He's *God!* Why can't he just *make* another angel? These people ...

NAT. Maybe God gives them comfort.

BECCA. Well, it pisses me off. Trying to find some ridiculous meaning in — "Hey look, I stepped in shit, it must be part of God's plan."

NAT. Now you're just being silly.

BECCA. *I'm* being silly.

NAT. Faith helps people cope. What's wrong with that? I know when your brother died —

BECCA. Again with Arthur.

NAT. If I didn't have God —

BECCA. See? That's *exactly* why I don't go: "If I didn't have God."

HOWIE. They're not all like that. Kevin's not. Gabby's not like that.

NAT. It sounds like you're jealous of their comfort.

BECCA. Yes, I *am*. Of *course* I am. How nice they all have something that makes them feel a little better. Like I don't feel bad enough, I've gotta go and have *that* rubbed in my face?

HOWIE. Nobody's rub — You're not being fair.

NAT. I don't know why you don't believe in God anyway.

BECCA. *(To Howie.)* You see? *Now* look where we're going!

NAT. I brought you to church every Sunday. You *used* to believe in God.

BECCA. Well, I don't anymore.

NAT. Well, you should. What if you're wrong? What if there *is* a God?

BECCA. Then I would say he's a sadistic prick.

IZZY.	NAT.	HOWIE.
Whoa, hey now ...	Becca, please.	Aw, jeez ...

BECCA. "Worship me and I'll treat you like shit." No wonder you like him, he sounds just like Dad.

NAT. You don't need to strike out at me, Becca. I know you're still in a bad place, but I'm trying to help you.

BECCA. Right.

NAT. I wish someone had sat me down when Arthur died. I wish someone gave me a little advice.

BECCA. You know what *I* wish?! *I* wish you would stop comparing Danny to Arthur! *Danny* was a four-year-old boy who chased his dog into the street! *Arthur* was a thirty-year-old *heroin* addict who *hung* himself! Frankly I resent how you keep lumping them together. *(Silence.)*

NAT. He was still my son.

BECCA. And I don't recall anyone giving you instructions on how best to grieve for him. *(Beat.)* I think it's time for me to go to bed now. *(Turns to her sister.)* Izzy, I hope you enjoy the bathroom set.

IZZY. I'm gonna. *(Becca heads upstairs. Izzy loads the dishwasher. Nat is still shaken by Becca's comment.)*

NAT. I was never that mean to anyone. When Arthur died, I was just as upset as she was, but I never took it out on other people like that.

IZZY. What about Mrs. Bailey?

NAT. *(Turns to her, annoyed.)* Nobody's talking about Mrs. Bailey. Izzy, please.

HOWIE. You know what this was about?

IZZY. *(Regarding Nat.)* Yeah, *her* and her mouth.

HOWIE. I knew the party was a bad idea.

IZZY. *(To Nat.)* Didn't I tell you not to get into anything with her?

HOWIE. We got a letter today. From Jason Willette. *(Beat.)*

NAT. What, why? What'd he want?

HOWIE. She said it didn't bother her but ... *(Regarding the gathering.)* Sorry, Iz.

IZZY. No, hey, this was *great*, really. Let's do it again *next* year. *(Crossfade to:)*

Scene 4

Later that night. Lights up on Danny's room. It looks essentially the same as it did when Danny was alive. The door opens and Becca enters. She doesn't come in here often. She quietly closes the door behind her. She looks around a bit, then takes a seat on Danny's bed. She takes a letter out of an envelope and rereads it. Lights up on Jason Willette, seventeen.

JASON. Dear Mr. and Mrs. Corbett, I wanted to send you my condolences on the death of your son, Danny. I know it's been eight months since the accident, but I'm sure it's probably still hard for you to be reminded of that day. I think about what happened a lot, as I'm sure you do, too. I've been having some troubles at home, and at school, and a couple people here thought it might be a good idea to write to you. I'm sorry if this letter upsets you. That's obviously not my intention. Even though I never knew Danny, I did read that article in the town paper, and was happy to learn a little bit about him. He sounds like he was a great kid. I'm sure you miss him a lot, as you said in the article. I especially liked the part where Mr. Corbett talked about Danny's robots, because when I was his age I was a big fan of robots, too. In fact I still am, in some ways — ha ha. I've enclosed a short story that's going to be printed in my high school lit magazine. I don't know if you like science fiction or not, but I've enclosed it anyway. I was hoping to dedicate the story to Danny's memory. There aren't any robots in this one, but I think it would be the kind of story he'd like if he were my age. Would it bother you if I dedicated the story? If so, please let me know. The printer deadline for the magazine is March 31st. If you tell me before then, I can have them take it off. *(Becca flips through the story enclosed.)* I know this probably doesn't make things any better, but I wanted you to know how terrible I feel about Danny. I know that no matter how hard this has been on me, I can never understand the depth of your loss. My mom has only told me that about a hundred times — ha ha. I of course wanted to say how sorry I am that things happened the way they did, and that I wish I had driven down a different block that day. I'm sure you do, too. Anyway, that's it for now. If you'd like to let me know about the dedication, you can email me at the address above. If I don't hear from you, I'll assume it's okay. Sincerely, Jason Willette. *(Beat.)* P.S. Would it be possible to meet you in person at some point? *(The lights slowly fade on Jason. Becca puts the story and letter aside. She just sits on the bed, taking in the room. Meanwhile, the lights rise on Howie in the living room. It's that same night. Nat and Izzy have gone home. Howie plunks into his chair and grabs a couple remotes. He clicks on the TV, then hits play on the VCR. We hear a documentary on tornadoes playing. Howie is confused. Something isn't right. He gets out of the chair and ejects the tape. He examines the tape, panic starts to set in. He pops the tape back in and hits play again. More tornado*

31

documentary.)

HOWIE. What is this? Becca? … Becca?! *(He hits fast-forward.)* *Becca?!*

BECCA. *(From upstairs.)* What?

HOWIE. What'd you do here?! *(The lights fade on Danny's bedroom. Howie keeps pressing fast-forward, but it's all tornadoes. He's beside himself. Becca comes running downstairs.)*

BECCA. What's the matter?!

HOWIE. What is this?!

BECCA. What's *what?!*

HOWIE. The *television.* What *is* this?

BECCA. *(Looks to TV.)* It's the Discovery Channel. The tornado program. You said you wanted to watch it. I recorded it for you. Why?

HOWIE. For *Chrissake!*

BECCA. What's the matter?

HOWIE. It's Danny's tape. You recorded over Danny's tape. *(Beat.)*

BECCA. No, I didn't. *Pride and Prejudice* was on that tape. We were watching it last night.

HOWIE. I switched them.

BECCA. *What?!*

HOWIE. I watched Danny's tape later. After you went to bed.

BECCA. Why didn't you take it out of the machine?!

HOWIE. Why didn't you check to see what was in there?!

BECCA. I assumed it was the TV tape!

HOWIE. Jesus, Becca!

BECCA. It was one of the baby videos?

HOWIE. No, it was the most recent, the long one. The park was on it, and Mexico —

BECCA. How was I supposed to know you snuck down here?

HOWIE. — and Christmas.

BECCA. I thought it was the TV tape.

HOWIE. It wasn't!

BECCA. I know, Howie.

HOWIE. So it's gone. The whole thing.

BECCA. I'm sorry.

HOWIE. It's the only copy, Becca!

BECCA. Well, I didn't do it on purpose.

HOWIE. Are ya sure? *(Beat.)*

BECCA. What does that mean? *(No response.)* You think I recorded over Danny's tape on purpose?

32

HOWIE. I don't know.

BECCA. You don't *know?*

HOWIE. I should've taken it out.

BECCA. Why would I deliberately record over it?

HOWIE. I don't know.

BECCA. Why *would* I?!

HOWIE. I don't *know!* (*Silence.*) You took the paintings off the fridge. Danny's paintings.

BECCA. To save them. I put them in plastic.

HOWIE. And shoved them in a box.

BECCA. For safekeeping.

HOWIE. Okay.

BECCA. I didn't throw the paintings out.

HOWIE. I know you didn't.

BECCA. You think I didn't want that tape?

HOWIE. I don't … Of course, you did. Obviously it wasn't on purpose, but —

BECCA. What?

HOWIE. Maybe subconsciously.

BECCA. Subconsciously. Is this what they're telling you at group? How I'm doing things subconsciously?

HOWIE. You're trying to get rid of him. I'm sorry, but that's how it feels to me sometimes. Every day, it's something else. It feels like you're trying to get rid of any evidence he was ever here. (*It's as if she's been slapped.*)

BECCA. I didn't know that tape was in there.

HOWIE. I'm not talking about the tape. Not just the tape.

BECCA. And the paintings are downstairs. In a box. You can look at them whenever you want.

HOWIE. The clothes. His shoes.

BECCA. We don't need all that stuff. Why would we keep — ?

HOWIE. Your wanting to sell the house!

BECCA. We already talked about —

HOWIE. Taz. Sending Taz to your mother's!

BECCA. There was a lot going on, Howie. We couldn't deal with the dog.

HOWIE. I was fine with the dog. *I* was the one walking him.

BECCA. Well, he got underfoot.

HOWIE. And he was a reminder.

BECCA. Yes, he was a reminder. So what? I wanted one less reminder around here. That's perfectly normal.

HOWIE. And since you never wanted the dog to begin with —

BECCA. Oh for godsakes —

HOWIE. Well, if I hadn't bought the dog —

BECCA. And if *I* hadn't run inside to get the phone, or if *I* had latched the gate —

HOWIE. *I* left the gate unlatched!

BECCA. Well, *I* didn't check it! *(Retreats a bit.)* I'm not playing this game again, Howie. It was no one's fault.

HOWIE. Not even the dog's.

BECCA. I *know* that.

HOWIE. Dogs chase squirrels. Boys chase dogs.

BECCA. Are you telling me or yourself?

HOWIE. He *loved* that dog!

BECCA. Of course he did.

HOWIE. And you got rid of him!

BECCA. Right, like I got rid of the tape. I get it.

HOWIE. *(Losing it.)* It's not just the tape! I'm not talking about the tape, Becca! It's Taz, and the paintings, and the clothes, and it's *everything!* You have to stop erasing him! You have to stop it! You HAVE TO STOP! *(Howie has been reduced to tears. He has to move away from Becca. She takes him in. She seems more confused than affronted.)*

BECCA. Do you really not know me, Howie? Do you really not know how utterly impossible that would be? To erase him? No matter how many things I give to charity, or how many art projects I box up, do you really think I don't see him every second of every day? And okay, I'm trying to make things a little easier on myself by hiding some of the photos, and giving away the clothes, but that does *not* mean I'm trying to *erase* him. That tape was an accident. And believe me, I will beat myself up about it forever, I'm sure. Like everything else that I could've prevented but didn't.

HOWIE. That's not what I want, Bec. It's not what I'm talking about.

BECCA. No? Because it feels like it is. It feels like I don't feel bad enough for you. I'm not mourning enough for your taste.

HOWIE. Come on, that's not —

BECCA. Or mourning in the right *way.* But let me just say, Howie, that I am mourning as much as you are. And my grief is just as real and awful as yours.

HOWIE. I know that.

BECCA. You're not in a better place than I am, you're just in a *dif-*

ferent place. And that sucks that we can't be there for each other right now, but that's just the way it is.

HOWIE. His stuff is all we have left. That's all I'm saying. And every bit of it you get rid of —

BECCA. I understand that. You don't wanna let go of it. I understand, Howie.

HOWIE. Do you? *(Beat.) Do* you? *(No response.)* This isn't … Something has to change here. Because I can't do this … like this. It's too hard. *(Beat.)* It's too hard. *(Neither speaks for a while. Then Howie heads for the stairs. He stops, and turns back to her.)* And I want that dog back. Your mother's making him fat. *(Beat.)* I want the dog back.

BECCA. Why don't we wait until —

HOWIE. I don't want to. How much more do we have to lose? *(Beat.)* I miss the dog. I'm sorry, but I miss him. I want him back. *(They regard each other silently. Howie heads upstairs, leaving Becca alone. The lights slowly fade.)*

ACT TWO

Scene 1

Living room. We hear a car pulling away as the lights rise on Howie, standing by the open front door, in a suit jacket, holding a clipboard for an open house. Two months have passed. It's early May. Izzy comes from the kitchen with a piece of torte. Her pregnancy is starting to show a little. She's four and a half months along.

IZZY. They were weird, huh? That last couple? The way they kept opening everything? Cabinets, closets …

HOWIE. It's an open house.

IZZY. Still, it was kinda nervy. I'd never do one of these things. Strangers strolling through, looking under my beds.

HOWIE. That's what you gotta do to sell a house.

IZZY. Well, lucky for me I'll never own a house then. *(Regarding torte.)* What is this, pie?

HOWIE. It's a torte.

IZZY. Is it good?

HOWIE. Yeah, it's good. *(Izzy settles in with the torte.)*

IZZY. We done?

HOWIE. Fifteen minutes. We're supposed to go till four. *(Looking over the sign-in sheet.)*

IZZY. How many'd ya get anyway?

HOWIE. Not many. No *serious* buyers. Maybe the German though. It's hard to tell.

IZZY. Is that what he was, German? I couldn't place the accent. I thought maybe Irish.

HOWIE. *Irish?*

IZZY. I couldn't tell.

HOWIE. We should probably get a broker. I think a lot of people are afraid of fisbos.

IZZY. Afraida who?

HOWIE. Fisbo: For Sale By Owner. No middleman. I was trying to avoid the commission but we probably need one. *(Regarding sign-in sheet.)* This was a wash I think. *(Looking over clipboard.)* I thought we had a bite with that family — the little girl. Nothing, though. Maybe I priced it too high. Or they were just browsing maybe.

IZZY. *(Eating.)* You freaked them out, Howie. *(Beat.)*

HOWIE. No, I didn't. What are you talking about?

IZZY. You should've cleaned out Danny's room. Made it look like a guest room or something. An office, or whatever.

HOWIE. Why?

IZZY. Because everyone that went in there was like, "Oh, you have a son, how old is he?" Did you think people wouldn't ask that?

HOWIE. I didn't think about it. I just thought it'd be good for them to see there was a nice room for a kid.

IZZY. But common sense, Howie. You've got these robot sheets on the bed, the conversation's gonna come up. And so everyone asks, and then you tell them, and then there's this weirdness in the air.

HOWIE. Only *two* people asked. That's all.

IZZY. Well, you ooged them out. If you had a kid, would you wanna move into a house where a boy just died? People believe in that stuff, you know. House karma, or whatever you wanna call it.

HOWIE. Well, they're stupid then.

IZZY. Yeah, they are. But if you wanna sell your house you gotta take that into consideration. I can't believe *I'm* giving *you* business advice.

HOWIE. Is that what this is?

IZZY. I'm just saying, sometimes you gotta sort out what is and isn't appropriate to say to people.

HOWIE. It isn't appropriate to talk about my son?

IZZY. Uh-uh, you're not pulling me into that conversation. You wanna tell total strangers all about Danny and how he died, it's none of my business. God knows it's something you enjoy doing, so you go ahead. But don't be surprised if nobody wants to buy your house. *(Finishes torte.)* Good God, Becca has gotta stop baking. I'm gynormous. *(We hear the dog barking out in the yard. Howie looks outside.)* Someone coming?

HOWIE. *(Regarding Taz.)* No, he's just mad he's still tied up.

IZZY. *(Looks at her watch, then.)* So, hey, let me ask you something … *(Beat.)*

HOWIE. All right.

IZZY. Why is Becca so mad at me? Is it just because I'm pregnant or …

37

HOWIE. Becca's not mad at you.

IZZY. Then why does she act so pissed at me sometimes?

HOWIE. I don't know. You should ask her.

IZZY. I can't.

HOWIE. Why not?

IZZY. Because that'll only make her *more* pissed.

HOWIE. Yeah, probably, but —

IZZY. Is it because she blames me? A little bit maybe?

HOWIE. Oh my God, Izzy …

IZZY. Because if I hadn't called to bitch about Mom she wouldn't have left Danny to run into —

HOWIE. Ten months later and you're asking me this?

IZZY. Well, I don't know.

HOWIE. No, Izzy. No. Nobody blames you.

IZZY. Okay. *(Beat.)* So it's just the baby then. The fact that I'm having a baby.

HOWIE. Honestly, I don't think Becca's mood has anything to do with you.

IZZY. She thinks I can't do it. Right? I'm not cut out to be a good mother?

HOWIE. She doesn't think that. You should *really* be having this conversation with her.

IZZY. I know I've been a fuck-up, but people get their shit together.

HOWIE. Of course they do.

IZZY. And maybe I'm not as organized as Becca, or homey, or whatever —

HOWIE. Nobody's comparing you.

IZZY. Really? Because that'd be a first.

HOWIE. Everyone's excited about the baby, Iz. But you gotta understand that there's other stuff going on around here.

IZZY. I'm not talking about the other stuff. I'm talking about me being a capable person who can raise a child, and look after it and protect it. I resent the feeling I get from her, and you too sometimes, honestly, that I don't *deserve* the baby. Or that I'm not mature enough, or smart enough or something, to take care of it. I mean, my God, if my mother could do it, how hard could it be? *(Beat.)*

HOWIE. You'd be surprised.

IZZY. Hey, that's not what I … I just want to feel like you guys have some faith in me, because I'm up to it.

HOWIE. Great. I hope you are.

IZZY. Oh, you *hope*. Thanks, Howie.

HOWIE. I don't know where you want this conversation to go. And I really don't know why you're having it with me. *(Glances at his watch.)* Aw, fuck it. Nobody's coming. *(Howie takes off his suit jacket. He tosses it onto the couch, then heads into the kitchen.)*

IZZY. Are you mad?

HOWIE. No.

IZZY. You seem mad.

HOWIE. *(From kitchen.)* I'm just getting a beer. You want one?

IZZY. No, I don't want a beer. *God. (Howie gets himself a beer out of the fridge, then reenters from the kitchen.)* Can I ask you something else?

HOWIE. What do you got, a list? "Things to ask Howie when he's cornered"?

IZZY. No. Not a *list*.

HOWIE. What is it?

IZZY. You're not gonna like it.

HOWIE. Well then, even better.

IZZY. Do you know my friend Reema?

HOWIE. This is the question?

IZZY. No, this is the prologue. You know how some books have prologues?

HOWIE. I'm familiar with the concept.

IZZY. That's Reema. You remember her?

HOWIE. Not really.

IZZY. I brought her to that barbecue like two years ago? Curly hair, kinda chubby.

HOWIE. Okay. I'll take your word for it.

IZZY. Well, Reema works at Calderone's. In New Rochelle. You know that restaurant? *(Beat.)*

HOWIE. Yeah.

IZZY. Well Reema, even though you don't remember her, remembers you pretty well from the barbecue, and she said she waited on you a couple weeks ago.

HOWIE. Did I stiff her on the tip? Because had I remembered her, obviously I would've —

IZZY. She said you were with a woman. *(Beat.)*

HOWIE. I was with another parent from the support group. Two weeks ago, right? We grabbed a bite after the meeting. If Reema had identified herself, I would've introduced them.

IZZY. Her husband doesn't attend the meetings?

HOWIE. Is this still part of the prologue?

39

IZZY. Why were you holding hands? *(Beat.)* Reema said you were holding hands.

HOWIE. And Reema's what exactly, your spy?

IZZY. No, she's a waitress. She was just at work. *You* were the one sneaking around.

HOWIE. Okay, now I *am* mad.

IZZY. I told you, you weren't gonna like it.

HOWIE. That woman is a friend of mine whose daughter died of leukemia six months ago. Jesus, Izzy, what are you trying to — ?

IZZY. I'm just asking a question. You don't have to get defensive.

HOWIE. Just because I was holding a person's hand doesn't mean —

IZZY. I know you and Becca are having troubles —

HOWIE. What are you *talking* about?

IZZY. — But I'd like to think that if things got to a point where they were unsaveable, that you'd be man enough to fish or cut bait —

HOWIE. Who said we were having troubles?

IZZY. — And not make things worse than they already are by fucking around behind Becca's back.

HOWIE. You are *way* off base, Izzy!

IZZY. And I know there's "other stuff going on around here," but that doesn't excuse it.

HOWIE. This is so beyond ridiculous, I don't even know how to respond to you.

IZZY. I don't need you to respond. I just wanted to ask the question and say what I had to say. You can do whatever you want about it.

HOWIE. About *what?* I'm not having an affair!

IZZY. Okay.

HOWIE. I was comforting a friend!

IZZY. Great, I'm glad to hear that.

HOWIE. And I don't know where this Reema person gets off making these offensive assumptions about me —

IZZY. She'll be happy to hear it was a misunderstanding.

HOWIE. I mean, God, Izzy. And right after your schpiel about *us* not having faith in *you.* What do you *think* of me?

IZZY. I'm sorry, it's my sister. I had to ask.

HOWIE. Well, you've asked.

IZZY. Indeed I have.

HOWIE. *Jesus. (Beat.)* I'll tell ya one thing, if I ever see this Reema *again,* I'm gonna tell her what I think of her talking shit about me.

IZZY. You should. She'll like that. *(Heads into the kitchen.)* I'm

40

gonna get some juice.

HOWIE. And for the record, I hope I *did* stiff her on the tip.

IZZY. Yeah well, for the record, you *did*. *(Left alone, Howie is reeling, but trying not to show it. He drinks his beer. After a couple beats, Becca and Nat come in through the front door carrying bags of groceries. They're in the middle of an argument.)*

NAT. Luckily she had read about it in the papers —

BECCA. Of course she did.

NAT. — So when I explained it, she realized who you were.

BECCA. You should've gotten her phone number. We could've had her over for cocktails.

HOWIE. Heyyy, they're back.

NAT. I was just trying to help.

BECCA. Well I don't need you chasing after me cleaning up my messes.

HOWIE. What happened?

BECCA. Or apologizing for me.

NAT. That's not what I was doing.

HOWIE.	IZZY.
Did something happen?	You get my message about the olive loaf?

BECCA. No, I shut my phone off.

NAT. I had to do *something,* Becca.

IZZY. *(To Becca.)* Why?

BECCA. *(To Izzy.)* Because you kept calling me.

IZZY.	NAT.
But I wanted olive loaf.	If I didn't say something, she would've had the cops there.

HOWIE. Cops where?

BECCA. She would not have called the cops.

NAT. You don't know that.

IZZY. Someone was gonna call the *cops?*

HOWIE. What *happened?!*

BECCA. Nothing.

NAT. We had a little scene, that's all. *(Regarding groceries.)* Lemme do this. *(Nat puts some of the groceries away. Becca moves to look over the sign-in sheet on the clipboard.)*

BECCA. How'd we do here? Looks a little light, doesn't it?

HOWIE. What kind of scene? What *scene* did you have?

BECCA. In the supermarket.

IZZY. You and Mom?

NAT. *(From the kitchen.)* No, I was not involved.

BECCA. It's so stupid.

HOWIE. What happened?

BECCA. This is why I hate shopping. Everything in there's like: "Oh look, Froot Loops, Danny liked Froot Loops. Hey, string cheese. Danny hated string cheese." Everything. Howie, you've got to do some of the food shopping. I'm sick of saying it.

NAT. *(Comes back in.)* Becca got a little upset.

HOWIE. About what?

NAT. There was a boy there.

HOWIE. He reminded you of Danny?

BECCA. No. Maybe a little, but not really, no.

NAT. He had red hair.

BECCA. What happened was we were in the same aisle as this kid and he wanted these roll-ups, fruit roll-ups, and his mother was being a hard-ass about it, saying she wasn't gonna buy them for him.

NAT. And it wasn't because she couldn't afford it, because you could tell she had money.

BECCA. But the kid was getting whiny about it. Which makes sense, because he's five years old and he really wants these roll-ups, but the mother wouldn't give in. In fact she starts ignoring him completely, just turns her face away and pretends he's not there. Just goes about her shopping, like that's gonna shut him up, or teach him a lesson or something. Case closed sort of thing. But that only gets him *more* upset. So that pissed me off for some reason.

HOWIE. What did?

BECCA. The way she was ignoring him, instead of trying to explain why he couldn't have them.

NAT. So she walked over to her.

HOWIE. What? Why?

BECCA. I don't know. I just did.

IZZY. What'd you say?

BECCA. I said, "It's only three bucks, why don't you just get him the fucking roll-ups?"

HOWIE. Oh, no …

BECCA. And she looked a little miffed. But she smiled a little — I don't know why — and explained to me that she didn't want her son eating candy. And so I said it wasn't actually candy, in fact fruit rollups are relatively healthy, and they're made with real fruit, and why not give him a treat? And she told me to mind my own busi-ness, and then tried to move her cart around me, but ran over my

foot by accident, so I smacked her. *(Beat.)*
HOWIE. What?
BECCA. I smacked her.
NAT. She did. She smacked her. I couldn't believe it. Real hard too.
HOWIE. Becca …
BECCA. I know. It was awful, and then the boy started crying. I felt terrible, but she pissed me off.
IZZY. You hit that woman?
HOWIE. Izzy, don't.
IZZY. I'm just saying. Glass houses.
BECCA. She was *ignoring* him.
NAT. She *was* ignoring him. It was pretty bitchy.
BECCA. I wanted to shake her: "Look at him. Don't pretend he isn't there!" But I didn't say that. I just stood there, kinda startled, and she was kinda startled, and then Mom came over and told me to go out to the car, which I did not need her to do.
NAT. I just explained everything to her. That's all I did. And she was mad at first, but I explained it, and she understood.
BECCA. No, she didn't.
NAT. After I talked with her, I'm saying.
BECCA. Still, she didn't understand, Mom. I'm sure you just made it seem like I was a crazy person. Some unstable —
NAT. You did slap her, Becca.
BECCA. She was lucky that was all I did! *(Nat shuts up about it, and goes back into the kitchen. Becca heads to the couch.)* Not that it helped. Not that she'll suddenly … realize … I mean, it was a *fruit roll-up.* Just let him *have* it. Am I wrong?
IZZY. No. I would've smacked her, too.
BECCA. Yeah, well, obviously. *(Beat.)* And I was doing well too, wasn't I, Howie? I had a bunch of good days in a row. *(Izzy snuggles up to her sister on the couch.)*
IZZY. You can come shopping with me anytime, Bec. I'm gonna give my kid whatever he wants. Candy, whatever.
BECCA. That wasn't my point, Izzy.
IZZY. No, I know, you're saying *be* with him. She blocked him out instead of … appreciating him, or whatever. I understand. I totally get it. And if you ever see me doing what she did, smack me, too, okay? *(Beat.)*
BECCA. Okay.
IZZY. Maybe you taught that lady something.
BECCA. Yeah, I don't think so.

IZZY. *(Calls off.)* Hey, Mom, did they have any Bosco?

NAT. *(From the kitchen.)* Right here.

IZZY. Oh good, let's crack that bad boy open. *(Heads off.)*

BECCA. *(Off Howie's look.)* What?

HOWIE. Nothing.

BECCA. Have I shocked you?

HOWIE. No. Not shocked, no.

BECCA. Well, you look shocked.

HOWIE. Do I?

BECCA. Or *something. (Taz starts barking. It immediately gets to Becca.)* Go quiet him down, wouldja, Howie? *(Howie turns to go. Jason is standing by the front door. He's entered, unnoticed. Pause. They all become aware of his presence. Nat and Izzy stand in the doorway of the kitchen.)*

JASON. Hello. Hi ... um ... I saw the sign outside, so ... the open house sign. And the door was open.

HOWIE. You looking to buy a house?

JASON. No.

BECCA. Howie —

HOWIE. What? He said he saw the sign.

JASON. I just wanted to say hey. *(Taz has not stopped barking.)*

HOWIE. Taz! Shut up! *(Taz stops barking. They all stare at Jason.)*

JASON. You know who I am, right?

HOWIE. Yeah, we know.

JASON. So, since the sign was out there, I thought it'd be okay if I just poked my head in. I've been wanting to say hello for a while and —

HOWIE. Now's not really a good time for us.

JASON. Oh. Okay.

HOWIE. We've got family visiting.

JASON. Right. I was just saying hey anyway. I didn't wanna bother you. Just say hello in person. But ... maybe another time would be better.

HOWIE. Yeah. It's just we have relatives here.

JASON. Right, you said. Hi.

IZZY and NAT. Hello.

JASON. Another time then.

BECCA. Yeah, we're ... we're around, so —

HOWIE. Becca ...

BECCA. What?

JASON. I could come by any afternoon really, if there's a day

44

you're —

HOWIE. Well, the problem is we're trying to sell the house, which takes up big blocks of our time.

JASON. It wouldn't take long. I just wanna sit down with you at some point.

HOWIE. Still —

JASON. I'd really like to arrange something if that's possible.

HOWIE. And I just told you now's not really a good time.

JASON. No, I know, but I wasn't talking about right now.

HOWIE. Great. So why don't you take off then? And if we can arrange something in the future we'll do that.

JASON. Okay. Well I wrote my number down … *(Pulls crumpled paper from his pocket.)* So if you free up at all … *(More awkward silence. He places the number on the closest piece of furniture. He's about to go, when:)*

HOWIE. Can I just say something to you? *(Advances on him.)*

BECCA.   NAT.   IZZY.
Howie, don't —   Hey, easy now.   Oh, Jesus.

HOWIE. An open house sign doesn't mean we're holding walking tours in here.

JASON. I know that.

HOWIE. You can't just pop in because the door's open. We were conducting business.

JASON. That's why I waited until that couple left. It looked like things were finished here.

HOWIE. Well, they're not.

JASON. Then I apologize.

HOWIE. We *live* here, okay? This is our *home.*

BECCA. All right, Howie. *(Reaches for his arm.)*

HOWIE. You don't just walk into someone's home like that. Especially given the *circumstances.* You should show a little respect.

JASON. I'm sorry. *(Looks to the others.)* I'm sorry I interrupted. *(Beat.)* Sorry. *(Jason exits. They're all silent for a couple beats.)*

HOWIE. You believe that? The balls on that kid? Walking in here?

NAT. *(Regarding laundry soap.)* I'm gonna bring this … *(Nat heads into the laundry room with the soap.)*

HOWIE. And what was he, out there hiding behind a tree or something? No wonder Taz was barking.

BECCA. Or maybe he was barking because he's hungry. Did you feed him?

HOWIE. Oh … no. I got caught up with —

45

.. No, of course not. You wanted that dog so badly, but you
.ver remember to feed him. *(Turns to go.)*
WIE. I'll do it.
.CCA. It's nice to know things are getting back to normal
.round here. *(Heads out back.)*
HOWIE. *(After Becca goes.)* That was the last thing she needed.
That kid showing up.
IZZY. She seemed fine with it. You were the one who got upset.
HOWIE. Yeah, well, I'm not the one slapping people.
IZZY. *(Regarding Jason.)* I don't know, you came pretty close just
then. *(Pause.)* So I'm free next week if you wanna try this again.
Another open house. *(Beat.)*
HOWIE. Maybe. We'll see.
IZZY. You really should do something about that room though.
Auggie does some renovation stuff on the side, if you want me to
ask him. He could get in there and —
HOWIE. Oh, I don't know …
IZZY. He does good work. He put up my mother's drywall.
HOWIE. I think we got it covered.
IZZY. Still, you should really try to fix things up a little. *(Beat.)*
The room, I mean.
HOWIE. Yeah, I know what you meant. *(Izzy heads into the kitchen,
leaving Howie alone. The lights fade.)*

Scene 2

*About a week later. Nat is helping Becca clean out Danny's
room. Becca is taking Danny's books out of a bookcase and
placing them into a milk crate. Nat is taking toys, stuffed ani-
mals, kids' puzzles, etc., out of a toy box and placing them into
a garbage bag or keep box.*

NAT. *(Holds up toy.)* Keep or toss?
BECCA. Toss.
NAT. *(Another.)* This too?
BECCA. Yeah. *(Nat puts both toys into the garbage bag. Becca finds
The Runaway Bunny. She flips through it.)* Remember this one?

(Holds up the book.)

NAT. That was *your* book.

BECCA. I know. *(Becca puts it in the keep box. Nat pulls a Curious George doll out of the toy box.)*

NAT. *(Holds it up.)* Monkey?

BECCA. Um, keep, I guess. *(She does.)*

NAT. Howie doesn't mind this?

BECCA. It was *his* idea. After that open house. Seems his grief goes out the window when it comes to maximizing profits. *(Beat.)* Sorry. I don't even know why I said that. Just being mean. *(They go back to work.)* Besides, it's not like we're getting rid of *everything.* *(Something stops Nat. She's holding a pair of Danny's sneakers. They're smaller than she remembers. Becca glances over at her and realizes what's happening. Simply:)* Don't do that. *(Takes the sneakers.)* Quick and clean, like a Band-Aid. *(Places the sneakers in a garbage bag.)* Otherwise we'll never get through it. *(Becca grabs a Kleenex from the bureau and passes it to Nat without missing a beat. She carries on as if the moment never happened.)* Did Izzy tell you I was taking a continuing ed. class? We're reading *Bleak House.* Isn't that hilarious? He handed out the syllabus and I just laughed. *Bleak House.* Of course no one knew what I was laughing at, which was *great. (Nat looks up at her.)* It's in Bronxville so no one knows me. I'm normal there. That's what I like best about it. I don't get "the face" every time someone looks at me.

NAT. What face?

BECCA. You know. *(Demonstrates, solemn pity.)* "Oh, hi. How ya doin'? Hangin' in there?" *(Nat laughs a little.)* I hate it. *(Together, they strip the robot sheets off the bed.)* And you know what's nice? These ladies don't even *talk* about their kids or their husbands or any of it. I think they're just so happy to be away from all that. It's probably the *last* thing they wanna talk about. Because I'm sure most of them are bored housewives, right?

NAT. I don't know. I've never met these people.

BECCA. Well, that's who takes Westchester continuing-ed classes, isn't it?

NAT. I guess.

BECCA. Sure, and they're just so happy to be talking about Dickens instead of what's for dinner. "Yay, we're reading literature." It's like they're in college again. Who'd *wanna* talk about their families? I know I don't. *(Beat.)* Anyway, I like it. I like that I'm just a lady taking a class. And next week we start *Madame Bovary.* That

47

oughta get the ol' girls goin', huh?

NAT. I don't know that book.

BECCA. No, I know. *(Nat, packing up more toys, accidentally flips the switch to an obnoxious yapping dog. It's loud.)*

NAT. What the hell? *(Trying to turn it off.)* How do I — ? *That's* annoying.

BECCA. *(Over the noise.)* Try listening to it for hours on end! *(Switches it off.)* Izzy gave him that. Only people without children give these kinds of gifts. Or people who want to punish parents. *(Then.)* You know what? Debbie's kids might like that. We should save it for *them*. That'd show her. *(Becca pops the toy into the keep box.)*

NAT. Still haven't heard from her?

BECCA. Nope. Howie plays squash with Rick but ... And I hear the kids are good. Do you remember Emily?

NAT. Of course.

BECCA. She's getting big now. *(Beat.)*

NAT. I thought you haven't seen them?

BECCA. No, but ... I passed by Danny's daycare last week, and the kids were all in the yard. *(Off her look.)* What? I was just walking by. That's how I get to the post office.

NAT. Yeah. Anyway, that's too bad about Debbie. But that can happen. Friends disappear. I remember when Arthur died — *(Stops herself.)* Sorry. *(Pause. Holds up a toy.)* What about this?

BECCA. No, it's busted. *(Takes it and tosses it.)*

NAT. You know, the thing about Debbie ...

BECCA. Yeah?

NAT. It's just as bad the other way sometimes. Do you remember Maureen Bailey?

BECCA. Sure.

NAT. Well I couldn't get rid of her after your brother passed away.

BECCA. I remember.

NAT. *Always* at the house. *Always* checking in on me. Eatin' up the cinnamon buns Uncle Jimmy brought me. I never had a moment to myself. And of course it was nice, I guess, but it didn't feel like it was about me. It just felt like she had nothing else to do. Like consoling me became her *hobby*. Something to fill up her day. And finally in the middle of coffee one afternoon, I said, "Maureen, why are you here all the time?"

BECCA. What'd she say?

NAT. She said, "I want to be there for you, Nat, I want to share in your grief." And so I said, "Well, it's not working. I seem to have

it all to myself still. You plant your fat ass in that c.a...
day — "
BECCA. You did not say that.
NAT. I did — "and suck up all my coffee, and I don't see you leav-
ing with any of this grief you're allegedly *sharing* with me. In fact
the only thing you *do* take outta here are my cinnamon buns."
(Beat.) So I never saw her again obviously. *(Beat.)* Which was too
bad actually, because she was the only one who was willing to talk
about Arth — *(Stops herself again.)*
BECCA. You can say his name.
NAT. Can I? I don't know your rules, Becca. I don't wanna get
scolded.
BECCA. You can talk about Arthur. I just don't like the comparisons.
NAT. Okay.
BECCA. It's not like the Arthur stuff didn't ... He was my brother,
so obviously that was a really hard time for all of us.
NAT. I know.
BECCA. But that was a long time ago, and it was very different.
For me.
NAT. Of course it was.
BECCA. Okay then. *(Back to work. Becca takes pictures off the wall.
Nat finds some papers on a bookcase.)*
NAT. What's this?
BECCA. Oh, it's a ... It's just a story that boy wrote. He sent it to
us.
NAT. *(Regarding the title.)* What is it, an *Alice in Wonderland* kind
of thing, or —
BECCA. No, it's more science fiction.
NAT. *(Turns a page.)* It's dedicated to Danny.
BECCA. Yeah, he asked if he could do that.
NAT. Why? It's about Danny?
BECCA. No, not at all. It's about a scientist.
NAT. Oh.
BECCA. Or the son of a scientist, actually. The father discovers
this warren of — It's like a network of holes to other galaxies, or
parallel universes, I guess, but he dies somehow. And so the son
goes into these holes trying to find him. Well, not *him,* because he's
dead, but another *version* of him.
NAT. It doesn't sound very good.
BECCA. It's okay. He's young.
NAT. Keep it?

every frickin'

...) Yeah, we should keep it. I'll just put it *...s the story inside the keep box. Nat goes back to ...templates telling her something, and finally relents. ...nd offhand.)* I think I'm gonna see him actually.

... no?

...CA. Jason Willette. *(Beat.)*

NAT. Why?

BECCA. I don't know. I just ... want to.

NAT. What about Howie?

BECCA. Howie's not really into it.

NAT. Well, I thought it was weird. The way he walked in like that. Creepy. You don't think that was creepy?

BECCA. Not really.

NAT. Well, I think it was creepy. You should ask Howie what *he* thinks.

BECCA. I don't have to ask him what he thinks. Frankly I don't care what he thinks.

NAT. I'm just saying. *(After a beat, Howie appears in the doorway. He looks around. The bed has been stripped. The walls are bare. He regrets popping in, but it's too late now.)*

BECCA. Hey.

HOWIE. How's it goin'?

BECCA. Fine.

HOWIE. Good. *(Beat.)* I thought we could put the brown bedspread in here.

BECCA. Okay.

HOWIE. And maybe hang the Ansel Adams prints that are in the basement?

BECCA. Sounds like a plan.

HOWIE. Making progress I see.

BECCA. Yup.

HOWIE. Good. Looks good. *(Pause.)* I'm gonna take Taz for a walk. You need anything while I'm out?

BECCA. I don't think so.

HOWIE. Okay. *(To Nat.)* Thanks for helping out, Nat.

NAT. Sure. *(He goes.)*

BECCA. *(Whispers.)* I hate that bedspread. I'm gonna put the blue one on. It's neutral enough. *(They work in silence. Nat suddenly smiles. She remembers something.)*

NAT. Hey, you know what I was thinking of this morning?

BECCA. What?

50

NAT. *(Chuckling a little already.)* Remember that gourmet basket you and Howie got me for Mother's Day last year, with the biscotti and the fancy biscuits? And I put the chocolates out when you came over for dinner, and Danny ate the entire bowl of chocolates when no one was looking?

BECCA. *(She's heard this story many times.)* Yup.

NAT. And then Howie was like, "Where'd all the chocolates go?" And I said, "Danny ate them. Leave him alone, kids like candy." And then Howie said, "But those were chocolate-covered espresso beans!" Remember?

BECCA. I do.

NAT. But Danny had eaten the whole bowl, so he was, you know, really really wired. And running in circles and climbing up the walls, and putting things on his head, and he was up until like three A.M. Remember that?

BECCA. Only too well.

NAT. I didn't know what the damn things were. I just thought they were candy. You get me these fancy baskets with all this crazy stuff in 'em — espresso beans. I tell that story to everyone. People get a kick out of it. *(Becca smiles.)*

BECCA. *(After a beat.)* Mom? *(Nat looks up at her.)* Does it go away?

NAT. What.

BECCA. This feeling. Does it ever go away? *(Beat.)*

NAT. No. I don't think it does. Not for me, it hasn't. And that's goin' on eleven years. *(Beat.)* It changes though.

BECCA. How?

NAT. I don't know. The weight of it, I guess. At some point it becomes bearable. It turns into something you can crawl out from under. And carry around — like a brick in your pocket. And you forget it every once in a while, but then you reach in for whatever reason and there it is: "Oh right. *That.*" Which can be awful. But not all the time. Sometimes it's kinda ... Not that you *like* it exactly, but it's what you have instead of your son, so you don't wanna let go of it either. So you carry it around. And it doesn't go away, which is ...

BECCA. What?

NAT. Fine ... actually. *(They're silent for a couple beats. Becca nods a little. She goes back to work. So does Nat. The lights fade.)*

Scene 3

A few days later. Jason is sitting on the couch in the living room. He looks around. Becca enters from the kitchen with a plate.

BECCA. I made some lemon squares. *(She holds out the lemon squares, and he takes one and a napkin.)*
JASON. Thank you.
BECCA. Can I get you milk or something? I don't have any soda. Unless you want seltzer.
JASON. I'm fine.
BECCA. You'll need something to wash it down, though. You don't drink coffee, do you?
JASON. Sometimes.
BECCA. You want coffee?
JASON. No thanks. Really, I'm okay.
BECCA. All right. But let me know if you change your mind. *(She joins him on the couch. Jason takes a bite of lemon square.)*
JASON. It's good.
BECCA. Thank you.
JASON. Still warm. *(She smiles. Pause.)* So, you're moving?
BECCA. We're thinking about it. If we can find a buyer.
JASON. Where are you moving to?
BECCA. We're still looking.
JASON. Far away?
BECCA. Probably not, no. My husband works in the city, so we can't go that far.
JASON. What does he do?
BECCA. He works at Prime Brokerage. Risk management.
JASON. *(Doesn't know what that is.)* Uh-huh.
BECCA. He takes the train in.
JASON. Right.
BECCA. So we don't wanna go too far.
JASON. It's a nice house. I hope you find one as nice as this.
BECCA. We'll probably go smaller. This is too big. *(Jason goes back to the lemon square.)* I'm sorry Howie couldn't be here.
JASON. That's okay.

BECCA. He's, uh …

JASON. Not ready?

BECCA. I was gonna say working, but yeah, *that* too.

JASON. He seemed mad. The other day.

BECCA. No, he was just surprised that you dropped by.

JASON. Okay.

BECCA. You just scared him a little bit.

JASON. He didn't seem scared.

BECCA. Yeah well … Maybe that's not the right word. But … Howie's not mad at you. What happened was an accident. Howie knows that. *(Beat.)* You know that, too, right? *(Jason takes a bite of lemon square. Taz barks out back. Becca cringes.)* That bark goes right through me. I swear, we better move somewhere without squirrels.

JASON. You should have his vocal cords snipped.

BECCA. What?

JASON. That's what some people do. If their dogs won't stop barking.

BECCA. Huh. I've never heard of that.

JASON. Yeah, because some dogs just never shut up. So that's what they have to do. Otherwise the alternative is give 'em away. Or put 'em to sleep, I guess. You should look it up online. I bet there's all sorts of information, if you're interested.

BECCA. No, Howie would never allow it. He loves that dog too much. *(Beat.)* Do you have any pets?

JASON. No.

BECCA. Well, that's lucky.

JASON. Yeah?

BECCA. Unless you *want* a pet. Do you want a pet? Because I've got one you can borrow. Just kidding. *(Pause. Jason notices a book on the coffee table.)*

JASON. We read that book.

BECCA. *Bleak House*?

JASON. Yeah, in English class.

BECCA. Did you like it?

JASON. Not really. It's too long.

BECCA. I know. I barely made it through.

JASON. I liked *David Copperfield* though.

BECCA. Also very long.

JASON. Yeah, but it didn't feel as long.

BECCA. No, you're right. *(Pause.)*

JASON. So, I don't see any photos anywhere.

BECCA. Of Danny?

JASON. Yeah.

BECCA. Well, we put most of them away. Because of the open house.

JASON. Okay.

BECCA. Do you *want* to see pictures? Because I could —

JASON. No thank you. *(Beat.)*

BECCA. Okay.

JASON. The one in the article was nice though. Him at the beach.

BECCA. That's at Anneport Bay.

JASON. I used to have a shirt just like that one. The one he's wearing in the picture. *(Beat.)* I might've been going too fast. That day. I'm not sure, but I might've been. So … that's one of the things I wanted to tell you. *(Beat.)* It's a thirty zone. And I might've been going thirty-three. Or thirty-two. I would usually look down, to check, and if I was a little over, then I'd slow down obviously. But I don't remember checking on your block, so it's possible I was going a little too fast. And then the dog came out, really quick, and so I swerved a little to avoid him, not knowing, obviously … *(Beat.)* So that's something I thought you should know. I might've been going a little over the limit. I can't be positive either way though. *(Pause.)*

BECCA. I'm gonna get you some milk. You don't have to drink it if you don't want it.

JASON. Okay. *(Becca heads into the kitchen. She gets a glass from a cabinet and fills it with milk.)*

BECCA. So you're a senior?

JASON. Yeah.

BECCA. Where you headed in the fall?

JASON. Connecticut College. They have a good writing program.

BECCA. Oh, well that's nice for you. And not too far from home. Your parents must be happy about that.

JASON. It's just my mom, but yeah, she's happy about it. She's already started picking out sheet sets for the dorm room.

BECCA. Uh-huh.

JASON. She keeps saying she's gonna apply to the graduate program so she can keep an eye on me while I'm up there. She's just joking though.

BECCA. Right.

JASON. She's not really looking forward to it, since I'm the only one at home now, but I told her I'd come back on the weekends when I could.

BECCA. That'll be nice. *(She reenters, brings him the milk.)* There ya go.

JASON. Thanks. *(He puts the milk down.)*

BECCA. And you graduate when?

JASON. Thursday. Matt Lauer is gonna speak. His niece is in my class.

BECCA. Well that's great. I like Matt Lauer.

JASON. Yeah. So does my mom.

BECCA. So you must have a prom coming up then.

JASON. It was last Saturday actually.

BECCA. And you went?

JASON. Yeah.

BECCA. Do you have a girlfriend or —

JASON. No. I mean, I *did,* but we broke up a while ago, so I went with this girl Carly who's just a friend, and this other girl Tina went with this guy Jake whose dad owns this old-fashioned Rolls-Royce that he brings to car shows and stuff, so we all went in that together.

BECCA. That must've been fun.

JASON. Yeah, it was a tight squeeze though, because no one wanted to sit up front, but it worked out. We had champagne in the back — not to get drunk or anything, just to celebrate — but Carly is really skinny so she got a little tipsy, even though she barely had like one glass of champagne. And she kept telling the driver to put the top down because she wanted to stand up in the back and act crazy, but the car wasn't even a convertible, so we essentially made fun of her all night for that. That part was pretty funny. *(Becca has been tearing up while listening. And with little warning, she is crying. A lot. It goes on for a few beats. Jason just sits, not sure what to do.)*

BECCA. I'm sorry.

JASON. No, that was stupid of me.

BECCA. I asked.

JASON. Still, I shouldn't have — Should I go?

BECCA. No. I'm fine. *(She collects herself. She grabs a Kleenex and blows her nose.)* I'm sorry. *(They sit in silence for a couple beats.)* So did you have a good time? At the prom?

JASON. It was okay.

BECCA. Well, it sounds like it was very nice. *(Beat.)* I liked that story you sent by the way. I'm sorry we never thanked you for it.

JASON. That's okay.

BECCA. We appreciated it. *(She grabs another Kleenex and wipes her nose.)* So the scientist that the boy is looking for …

JASON. Yeah?

BECCA. Is that your dad? *(Beat.)*

JASON. No.

BECCA. I mean, is it based on him?

JASON. No. My dad was an English teacher.

BECCA. Oh. Okay. I was just curious about that part. He is dead though, right?

JASON. It's just a story.

BECCA. No, I know. I'm sorry. It's none of my business. I was just ...

JASON. Reading into it?

BECCA. Yeah. *(Beat.)* Well, anyway, I liked it very much. It reminded me of Orpheus and Eurydice. Do you know that Greek myth?

JASON. Not really.

BECCA. Eurydice dies, and Orpheus misses her so much, that he travels to Hades to retrieve her, but in the end it doesn't work out.

JASON. I should read it.

BECCA. Yeah, it's similar. But instead of Hades, you have the rabbit holes. The parallel universes. It's interesting. I liked that part.

JASON. Thank you.

BECCA. Is that something you believe in?

JASON. Parallel universes?

BECCA. Yeah.

JASON. Sure. I mean, if space is infinite, which is what most scientists think, then yeah, there *have* to be parallel universes.

BECCA. There *have* to be?

JASON. Yeah, because infinite space means ... it means it goes on and on forever, so there's a never ending stream of possibilities.

BECCA. Okay.

JASON. So even the most unlikely events have to take place *somewhere,* including other universes with versions of us leading different lives, or maybe the same lives with a couple things changed.

BECCA. And you think that's plausible.

JASON. Not just plausible — probable. If you accept the most basic laws of science.

BECCA. Huh. *(Beat.)* So somewhere out there, there's a version of me — what? — making pancakes?

JASON. Sure.

BECCA. Or at a water park.

JASON. Wherever, yeah. Both. If space is infinite. Then there are tons of you's out there, and tons of me's.

BECCA. And so this is just the sad version of us. *(Beat.)*

JASON. I guess.

BECCA. But there are other versions where everything goes our way.

JASON. Right. *(Beat. A change.)*

BECCA. And those other versions *exist.* They're not hypothetical, they're actual, *real* people.

JASON. Yeah, assuming you believe in science.

BECCA. Well that's a nice thought. That somewhere out there I'm having a good time.

JASON. *(After a pause.)* So, could you tell your husband for me? How I might've been going a little over the limit? I know he's probably still mad but —

BECCA. He's not mad. Nobody's mad.

JASON. Okay. *(Beat.)* Can you tell him though? *(Beat.)*

BECCA. Sure. *(Jason goes for the milk. He drinks it as the lights fade.)*

Scene 4

Eat-in kitchen. Dusk. Nat enters with a box of toys and books from Danny's room. She places them on the table. Izzy follows, reading The Runaway Bunny.

IZZY. I don't remember *The Runaway Bunny* being so weird. The mother's like a stalker.

NAT. Oh, come on. She's not a stalker.

IZZY. Well, of course *you* don't think so. But look, she turns into wind and shit, a mountain climber. Poor kid needs to get himself a restraining order. *(Izzy puts the book in the box, and finds the obnoxious yappy dog toy she had given to Danny.)* Heyyy, I remember this. She said I could have it?

NAT. Oh, yes, that one *especially* she wants you to have. *(Becca enters with a recipe she's printed out for Izzy.)*

BECCA. Here. I typed it all out for you. I put down lime zest in the filling, but you can also use orange zest, or even a little grapefruit. Or lemon, obviously.

IZZY. *(Looking at the recipe.)* Jesus. It's like three pages long. This looks hard, Becca.

BECCA. It's not. I promise. I put everything down.

IZZY. I hope the oven works. I don't think Auggie's ever used it. He keeps dishes in there.

BECCA. If you get stuck, you can call me.

IZZY. Okay. *(Beat. Chuckles.)* Me — baking. Auggie's gonna be shocked.

NAT. Well, anyone in their right mind *would* be.

IZZY. Ha ha. *(Howie enters, home from work, calling as he enters:)*

HOWIE. Hello-hellooo ... *(He's carrying something in tinfoil. Becca is surprised to see him.)*

IZZY. Hey, Howie.

NAT. Hello.

HOWIE. Hi.

BECCA. You're home.

HOWIE. *(Taking off his jacket.)* Yeah.

BECCA. I thought you had group.

HOWIE. I decided to skip it. *(Beat.)*

IZZY. Mom, we should get going, if you wanna get to bingo.

NAT. Why, what time is it?

IZZY. We gotta *go.* Auggie wants me to register for Lamaze, so I can learn how to shove a baby out of my body. *(Regarding box of toys.)* Thanks for the stuff.

BECCA. You're welcome.

IZZY. Bye, Howie.

NAT. *(To Becca.)* Bye, sweetie.

HOWIE. Bye, guys. *(As they exit with the box of stuff ...)*

NAT. Bingo's just at Saint Catherine's, you know. What's the bum's rush for?

IZZY. Can we talk about this in the car please?

NAT. I didn't even get a lemon square. *(And they're gone.)*

HOWIE. *(Regarding tinfoil.)* Alan brought in his zucchini bread again. He made me take what was left. He wants you to try it.

BECCA. That was nice of him. You'll have to thank him for me. *(Howie gets himself a beer.)* We had paillard if you're hungry. It's in there.

HOWIE. No, Alan kept pushing that bread on me all day.

BECCA. Okay.

HOWIE. *(After a couple beats.)* So how'd it go with the kid?

BECCA. Fine. It was totally fine.

HOWIE. What'd he want?

BECCA. Just to ... I don't know, introduce himself, I guess, talk a little.

HOWIE. Did you let him off the hook?

BECCA. What do you mean?

HOWIE. Well, he seemed pretty intent on sitting down with us. I assumed he wanted to be absolved or something. *(No response.)* Is that what he wanted?

BECCA. Not really. Not in so many words, no.

HOWIE. Huh. Did you tell him we didn't blame him?

BECCA. We *don't* blame him.

HOWIE. No, I know, but did you let him know that?

BECCA. I guess so. *(Beat.)*

HOWIE. That's good. *(Beat.)* So I don't have to meet him then, do I?

BECCA. Not if you don't want to, no.

HOWIE. Okay. *(He sits at the table.)*

BECCA. Why aren't you at group?

HOWIE. I just decided to skip it tonight. Wasn't up to it.

BECCA. How come?

HOWIE. I think I might be done. With the group. I don't think I'm gonna go back.

BECCA. Why, what happened?

HOWIE. Nothing. I just don't think it's as helpful to me anymore. I wanna try it on my own for a while. I mean, not on my own, obviously, but … without the group. *(Beat.)* That sound okay?

BECCA. Sure. If you're not getting anything out of it, then why go?

HOWIE. Exactly. *(Beat.)*

BECCA. Are you okay?

HOWIE. Yeah. I'm just tired. And full of zucchini bread.

BECCA. All right. I'm gonna have a piece. It's good?

HOWIE. Yeah, it's great. *(Becca goes to cut a piece of the zucchini bread.)*

BECCA. So Rick and Debbie invited us over for a cookout this weekend. *(Beat.)*

HOWIE. Really?

BECCA. Sunday they said. Are you free?

HOWIE. Yeah. You talked to Rick?

BECCA. No. Debbie.

HOWIE. You talked to Debbie.

BECCA. Yeah. I called her.

HOWIE. Wow. She must've been surprised.

BECCA. She was.

HOWIE. What'd she say?

BECCA. Oh you know, she cried mostly, and then apologized about sixty times, and then cried some more.

HOWIE. Sounds great.

BECCA. It was okay. She said she kept meaning to call, but she felt freaked out about everything and so she kept putting it off, and before she knew it months had gone by, and so then she *really* couldn't call because she felt like such an asshole, and assumed I hated her, so it just seemed easier to not pick up the phone.

HOWIE. And that was good enough for you?

BECCA. I don't know. Probably. We'll see how the barbecue goes. *(She joins him at the table.)*

HOWIE. Are the kids gonna be there?

BECCA. Of course. *(Beat.)*

HOWIE. That'll be hard.

BECCA. Yeah. It'll be good to see them though. We should get something for Emily. We missed her birthday. She turned four last week.

HOWIE. Right. Okay. *(Beat.)* Danny's is coming up.

BECCA. I know.

HOWIE. That's gonna be a tough one.

BECCA. Yeah. *(Silence as Becca eats the bread. Regarding zucchini bread:)* It's good.

HOWIE. I'll tell Alan you liked it. *(More silence.)* It's so quiet.

BECCA. That's because I slipped Taz a couple Ambien.

HOWIE. *(Smiles.)* You're funny.

BECCA. You think I'm joking. *(Becca takes another bite of zucchini bread. After a beat:)* You think we should reconsider the house? *(Beat.)*

HOWIE. If nobody bids, we might have to.

BECCA. There are worse things, I guess.

HOWIE. Yeah.

BECCA. It's a nice house.

HOWIE. I know.

BECCA. *(After a pause.)* So what are we gonna do?

HOWIE. About what?

BECCA. I don't know, pick something.

HOWIE. Well … *(Thinks it over.)* We could go to Village Toys tomorrow and pick up Candy Land for Emily. That's probably something she'd like.

BECCA. Okay, Candy Land. That's a start. Then what?

HOWIE. Then we wrap it.

BECCA. Uh-huh.

HOWIE. And then on Sunday we go to the cookout, and we give her the gift, and we talk to Rick and Debbie, and to make them feel comfortable we ask the kids a bunch of questions about what they've been up to, and we'll pretend that we're really interested. And then we'll wait for Rick and/or Debbie to bring up Danny while the kids are playing in the rec room. And maybe that'll go on for a little while. And after that we'll come home. *(Beat.)*

BECCA. And then what? *(Beat.)*

HOWIE. I don't know. Something though. We'll figure it out.

BECCA. Will we?

HOWIE. I think so. I think we will. *(Silence. They just sit for several beats, not even looking at each other. They're scared. Then Becca takes Howie's hand. They hold on tight. And the lights slowly fade.)*

End of Play

PROPERTY LIST

Laundry
Orange juice, glass
Crème caramels, knife, plates, spoons
Wine, glasses
Toy dinosaur
Children's book
Videotapes
Remotes
Birthday cake with candles, knife, plates, forks
Papers
Dictionary
Gift-wrapped bath set
Gift certificate
Plastic wrap
Letter
Clipboard
Torte
Beer
Bags of groceries, laundry soap
Paper
Books, toys, clothes, moving boxes, garbage bag
Sneakers
Tissues
Lemon squares, plate
Glass of milk
Book
Zucchini bread in tinfoil

SOUND EFFECTS

Dryer buzz
Videotape of child and dog
Videotape of tornado documentary
Car pulling away
Dog barking

AUTHOR'S NOTE

Rabbit Hole is a delicate play tonally, and its balance can be easily thrown out of whack. With that in mind, a little guidance from the playwright …

Yes, *Rabbit Hole* is a play about a bereaved family, but that does not mean they go through the day glazed over, on the verge of tears, morose or inconsolable. That would be a torturous and very uninteresting play to sit through. The characters are, instead, highly functional, unsentimental, spirited, and often funny people who are trying to maneuver their way through their grief and around each other as best they can. Sure, they hit bumps along the way, and are overcome by various emotions, but I've tried to be very clear about exactly when and how that happens.

It's a sad play. Don't make it any sadder than it needs to be. Avoid sentimentality and histrionics at all costs. If you don't, the play will flatten out and come across as a bad movie-of-the-week.

Tears — If the stage directions don't mention tears, please resist adding them. Howie gets some at the end of Act One. Becca cries at one point during her scene with Jason. Nat might *almost* cry when she finds Danny's shoes in his room. But I think that's about it. I'm pretty sure Izzy doesn't need to cry in this play. And I *know* Jason shouldn't cry, ever. (Yes, he's haunted by the death of Danny, but his emotions aren't especially accessible to him. Please, no choked-up kids openly racked with guilt. That's not who he is. Restraint, please.)

Laughter — There are, I hope, many funny parts in the play. They are important. Especially to the audience. Without the laughs, the play becomes pretty much unbearable. Don't ignore the jokes. They are your friends.

Please, no extra embracing, or holding of hands. Avoid resolution at all costs. Becca and Nat, for example, shouldn't hug at the end of their scene in Danny's room. It's not that kind of play. There can and should be moments of hope and genuine connection between these characters, but I don't ever want a moment (not even the very end) where the audience sighs and says, "Oh good, they're gonna be okay now." *Rabbit Hole* is not a tidy play. Resist smoothing out its edges.